CHRISTIAN HEROES: THEN & NOW

# JOHN NEWTON

## Change of Heart

Christian Heroes: Then & Now

# JOHN NEWTON

## Change of Heart

JANET & GEOFF BENGE

YWAM Publishing
Seattle, Washington

YWAM Publishing is the publishing ministry of Youth With A Mission (YWAM), an international missionary organization of Christians from many denominations dedicated to presenting Jesus Christ to this generation. To this end, YWAM has focused its efforts in three main areas: (1) training and equipping believers for their part in fulfilling the Great Commission (Matthew 28:19), (2) personal evangelism, and (3) mercy ministry (medical and relief work).

For a free catalog of books and materials, call (425) 771-1153 or (800) 922-2143. Visit us online at www.ywampublishing.com.

**John Newton: Change of Heart**


Published by YWAM Publishing
a ministry of Youth With A Mission
P.O. Box 55787, Seattle, WA 98155-0787



Cataloging-in-Publication Data is on file at the Library of Congress.

ISBN 978-1-57658-909-0 (print)
ISBN 978-1-57658-656-3 (e-book)

Second printing 2023

Printed in the United States of America

## Christian Heroes: Then & Now

Adoniram Judson
Albert Schweitzer
Amy Carmichael
Betty Greene
Brother Andrew
Cameron Townsend
Charles Mulli
Clarence Jones
Corrie ten Boom
Count Zinzendorf
C. S. Lewis
C. T. Studd
David Bussau
David Livingstone
Dietrich Bonhoeffer
D. L. Moody
Elisabeth Elliot
Eric Liddell
Florence Young
Francis Asbury
George Müller
Gladys Aylward
Helen Roseveare
Hudson Taylor
Ida Scudder
Isobel Kuhn
Jacob DeShazer
Jim Elliot
John Flynn
John Newton
John Wesley
John Williams
Jonathan Goforth
Klaus-Dieter John
Lillian Trasher
Loren Cunningham
Lottie Moon
Mary Slessor
Mildred Cable
Nate Saint
Norman Grubb
Paul Brand
Rachel Saint
Richard Wurmbrand
Rowland Bingham
Samuel Zwemer
Sundar Singh
Wilfred Grenfell
William Booth
William Carey

*Available in paperback, e-book, and audiobook formats.Unit study curriculum guides are available for select biographies.*

*www.YWAMpublishing.com*

# North Atlantic Ocean

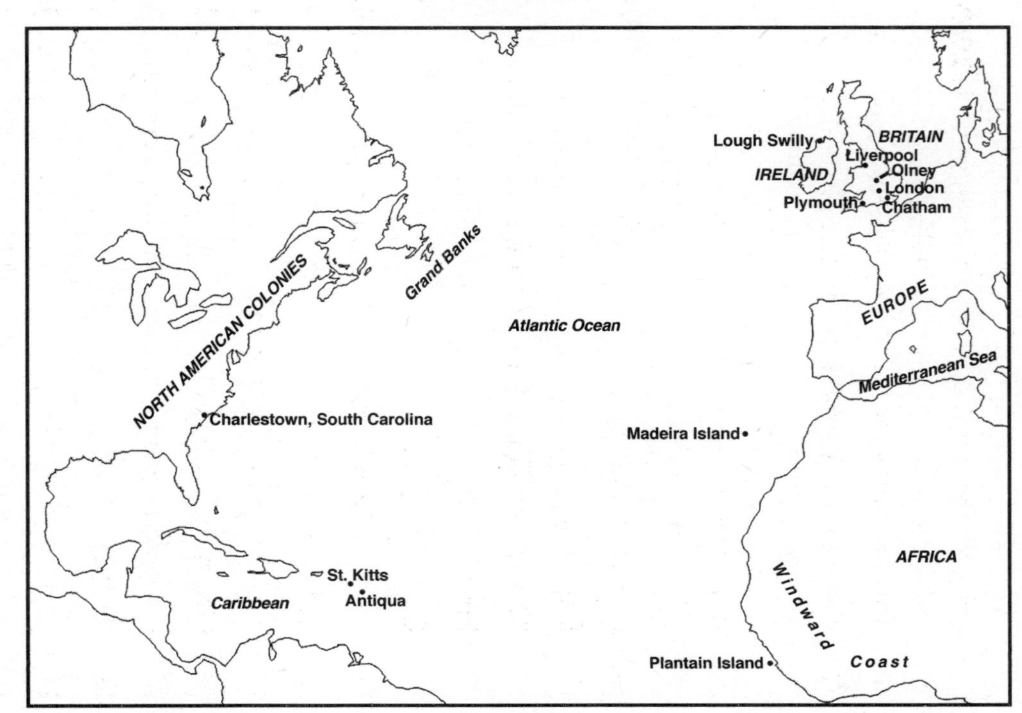

## Contents

## Chapter 1

# Things Had Gone Terribly Wrong

John Newton scrambled to his feet and stumbled into the field behind the row of slave huts, where he fell to the ground. He clumsily pulled up a root and took a bite. Even though it tasted bitter and coated the inside of his mouth with dirt, his hunger drove him on. As he kept eating, the gnawing pangs in his stomach began to let up. By then John knew he had to get back to the hut. As he tried to stand up, his head spun and he started to vomit.

After stumbling back to the hut, he fell onto the woven mat he called a bed. John was exhausted from the effort of finding food and discouraged that his stomach had rejected the roots he risked everything foraging for. But as he lay in the darkness, he realized that his gnawing hunger had subsided.

The next night John stumbled back to the field and ate more roots, which he again vomited up. But once more, for several hours afterward, he felt full. He continued again the next night, and the night after that. Yet John knew that vomiting up all he ate was not going to keep him alive. He needed nourishing food, something the plantation owner's wife seemed not to want him to have. She appeared willing to let him die of starvation.

The other slaves, black men and women from deep in the heart of Africa, took pity on John. After dark, some of them, shackled together in leg irons, sneaked into his hut and shared a portion of their meager water and food rations with him. As he ate, it occurred to John that he, an Englishman, was worse off than even the slaves living on the island. Things weren't supposed to be this way. He'd planned to make a fortune with which to return home to England. He would be set up for life. He was going to sweep Polly Catlett off her feet, and the two of them would live a happy life together in a large stone house in the countryside. But things had gone terribly wrong. Here he was, enslaved on a tiny island along the Windward Coast of West Africa, barely clinging to life. In his near delirious state, John wondered how things might have turned out differently for him if he'd made some better choices back when he had the chance.

Chapter 2

# His Hopes Were Dashed

Six-year-old John Newton stood on the doorstep of his house on Red Lyon Street staring at the hackney carriage as it turned right onto Green Bank Road. Then it was gone. Inside the horse-drawn carriage was his mother, Elizabeth. In his head, John went over the events of the day, trying to make sense of what was happening. He knew his mother was sick. She had been sick on and off for as long as he could remember. He was used to her lying in bed during the day as she instructed him in Latin or listened as he recited the Assembly's Shorter Catechism or some of Isaac Watts's *Divine Songs for Children*. John knew that his mother also loved to hear him recite poetry. Sometimes she would have long coughing spells, after which her cheeks would be flushed. Once John had overheard his mother tell their pastor, Dr. David Jennings, that she had consumption, though he didn't know exactly what that meant.

Yesterday Elizabeth Catlett, a distant cousin of John's mother, had visited. She took one look at his mother and announced she needed some sea air if she was to have any hope of recovery. John knew that the air in Wapping, located beside the Thames River on the edge of London, was thick with smoke and acrid smells. A hundred or more workshops and factories, including potteries, dye works, gunsmiths, and blacksmiths, lined the riverfront, their chimneys belching black smoke into the air. In winter, smoke from these factories, along with the smoke from household fireplaces, combined with fog to wrap Wapping in a pall of grayness, through which the sun rarely pierced. John knew that breathing fresh air, especially the air nearer the sea, such as in Chatham, Kent, where the Catletts lived, could be good for his mother.

At first John assumed he would be making the trip to Kent with his mother. But his hopes were dashed when Elizabeth Catlett arranged for him to stay with a member of the church while his mother went off to Kent. And now she was gone. The woman John had spent every day of his life with, who'd taught him to read when he was three years old, who had been his only teacher, playmate, and confidante, had been wrapped in a woolen shawl, propped up in a carriage, and taken from him.

Over the next two weeks John found that the rhythm of life went on. He helped fetch water from the well at the end of the street and watched over the younger children in the house. To please his mother, he continued learning large portions of the Westminster Shorter Catechism by heart and reading Isaac Watts's *A Short View of the Whole of Scripture History*. John prayed for his father, a ship's captain who was currently away on a voyage. On Sundays, he attended the Old Gravel Lane Independent Meetinghouse on Prince's Square. It was a Dissenter chapel, where Dr. Jennings preached each Sunday.

Most of the time Dr. Jennings's sermon was too hard for John to understand, but John loved the new hymns Isaac Watts introduced to the congregation. Isaac lived nearby in Stoke Newington and was a friend of Dr. Jennings. He sometimes came to the Dissenter chapel to teach the congregation one of his new songs. John's favorite new hymn introduced by Isaac Watts was "When I Survey the Wondrous Cross." This hymn had a jaunty tune that sounded to him more like a sailor's shanty than the droning psalms chanted at Saint John's, Wapping's official Anglican church, which John attended with his father when he was home.

After John had done his chores and completed his studies, he had not much else to do. He spent hours walking along the riverfront, from where he could see the roof of the nearby Tower of London. His mother had told him that this was where King George II kept the crown jewels. John loved to stand at the top of Wapping Stairs, the stone stairs that led from the end of the street down to the north bank of the Thames.

From there he would watch the bumboats ferry supplies of food, water, paint, and sailcloth to the ships moored along the river. Meanwhile longboats jostled as they brought sailors ashore and picked up others. But best of all, John liked to stare at the hundreds of tall ships lying at anchor, waiting for the right tide to set sail for some foreign port.

At times John's mother wouldn't let him go near the Wapping Stairs, mostly when a pirate was being executed by hanging. The gallows were set up beside the stairs, and the pirate, or group of pirates, was hung from a short rope. The short rope meant that the pirate did not die straightaway.

Huge crowds would gather to watch the spectacle. Then, as an extra warning to anyone who might think being a pirate was a fast way to riches, the dead bodies were left dangling in the water for a day and a half until three tides had washed over them. After this, the bodies were taken from the end of the rope and buried in a pauper's grave in Saint John's Cemetery, just a few yards up the street. It was sobering for John to think about, especially with his father away at sea. Pirates were just one more thing for John to concern himself about while his father was gone.

Although Wapping was thirty-five miles from the sea, it was the eastern extension of the bustling port of London. Each year thousands of ships from as far away as Jamaica, India, and other exotic locations unloaded sugar, rum, rice, tea, tobacco, spices, fine china, and cotton fabrics. When a ship had been unloaded, it was then reloaded with bales of English wool, tools, paper, and furniture to be carried to far-off ports.

On July 13, 1732, John received the terrible news that his mother had died. He could barely take in the fact that he would never see her again. Dr. Jennings and his wife visited John. They brought with them black crêpe fabric to drape over the windows and doors of the Newton house. John was allowed inside the house to collect a few of his possessions before it was locked up again to await his father's arrival.

John waited for his father with a sense of dread. The two of them had never been close. Captain John Newton was a stern, humorless man who didn't know how to talk to young boys. He preferred to bark out orders at home just as he did when commanding a ship at sea. When Captain Newton arrived home in Wapping from his extended voyage in the Mediterranean, he had no idea his wife had died, though he appeared to show little emotion when he found out. John didn't expect his father to comfort him over losing his mother. He hoped the man would just let him alone.

Within weeks of his return, John's father came home and announced he was getting married again, this time to a woman named Thomasina, a farmer's daughter. John was astonished, and even more so when he learned that Thomasina didn't want to live in London. John's father had agreed to sell the Wapping house and move to the countryside to live with his new wife. And John, now seven years old, was going with him. A thousand questions ran through

John's mind: Where had his father met Thomasina? What would he do in the country? Would he be able to continue his lessons? Of course, because he knew that asking his father such questions would only make him angry, John packed up his few belongings and boarded a coach with his father bound for Aveley, fifteen miles east of Wapping, in Essex.

John, a city boy, had never been to the countryside before. As John and his father left London behind, and green fields dotted with cows and sheep emerged beside the road, John had serious doubts he would ever adjust to living in the country. They arrived in Aveley, where John met his new stepmother. He was amazed by how young she was.

After greeting John, Thomasina paid little attention to him. She lived on her father's farm, and John was given a list of farm chores to do each morning, including milking the cow and feeding the pigs. It didn't take John long to realize he hated being a farm boy. He longed for the excitement of a bustling port.

Although he now lived on a farm in the Essex countryside, it was only a few miles from the Thames River. John soon discovered that if he climbed a nearby oak tree he could glimpse the tall masts of ships in the distance beyond the Essex marshes. Each time he saw the masts, unfurled sails and flags flapping in the breeze, John felt pangs of homesickness for his old neighborhood, his old house, his old church, but most of all his mother.

John soon learned that Thomasina was very different from his own mother. She could not read or write and had no interest in helping him find someone to teach him his lessons. Nor was she a praying woman, and she was unimpressed by the fact that John could recite religious catechisms, hymns, and poems by heart. In Aveley the family seldom went to church, and when they did, it was to an Anglican church, which was far from the lively Dissenter church John had enjoyed attending with his mother. John tried hard to hold onto the ideas his mother had taught him. She had always told him she wanted him to go to Saint Andrew's University in Scotland to train as a clergyman when he grew up. But with each passing month on the farm, that vision grew dimmer.

It wasn't too long before Captain Newton went back to sea, leaving John alone with virtual strangers. John barely spoke to his stepmother and worked through his chores as quickly as possible. Since there was no one to teach him his lessons, when he was done with his chores, he roamed the hills around Aveley. In autumn he gathered blackberries and fished in a nearby stream. Slowly he made friends with some of the other boys on nearby farms.

Soon after John turned eight years old, his father returned from his sea voyage and came to stay on the farm. This time Captain Newton took more notice of John, or at least his lack of schooling. Before he knew it, John was sent off to a boarding school in Stratford, twenty miles away. At first, John was happy about this move, until he realized that the headmaster of the boarding school was a tyrant. Nothing John or the other students did could please him. He lashed out at the boys with a whip and mocked them when they tried to answer questions. John was shocked. He had never encountered anyone who was so cruel to children. His desire to learn evaporated, turning instead into a desire to make it through the school year with as few beatings as possible.

Since the students at the school lived in the headmaster's house, they had no place to escape. John was forced to study for hours a day without any breaks for games or play. Sunday was the only day the routine differed, and that time was spent attending a church service once and chapel service twice. All thoughts had to be "pious," and reading anything other than the Bible was forbidden.

At the end of the school year, John went back to his stepmother on the farm for the summer holiday. He returned to the boarding school in early autumn for a second year. Much to his relief, the previous headmaster had been replaced by a more reasonable man, who was also a good tutor. John studied hard under him and did well, especially in Latin, where he read two classic writers, Cicero (also known as Tully) and Virgil.

By 1735, John had completed two years of study at boarding school. He was almost ten years old and still carried the hope of attending Saint Andrew's University. However, his father decided he'd paid for enough education for his son and instead pulled John from school. John's formal education was over. Captain Newton had a different plan for his only son. John would join him on his ship at sea, where he would serve as a cabin boy.

On his tenth birthday, carrying a duffel bag containing a change of clothes and several books, John followed his father up the gangplank of his ship moored off Purfleet Jetty on the Thames. The ship was bound for Spain with a shipment of corn. It was a new chapter in John's eventful life, and he had no idea what lay ahead.

Chapter 3

# Cabin Boy

For as long as he could remember, John had tried to imagine what his father's life at sea was like, and now he was about to find out. Once aboard ship, John was fascinated by all the activity around him as the crew prepared to set sail. Then came the shouts of sailors as the ropes mooring the ship to the dock were let go. The vessel drifted out into the current, and the sails were unfurled and billowed in the wind as they started moving on the outgoing tide. John watched his father bark orders as the ship sailed down the remaining twelve miles of the twisting Thames River, passing Gravesend and out into the open sea. Sea spray whipped over the ship's bow as it cut through the waves.

Most sailors got sick the first time they encountered the continuous rolling motion of a ship on the sea, but not John. The young sailor kept his food down and was declared to be a "natural sailor with good sea legs." Despite being declared a natural sailor, John soon learned that as cabin boy he didn't have the luxury of standing idly on the deck, even if he was the captain's son. His job was to do the lowest tasks aboard ship. He helped the cook ladle out rations of salted pork from a huge barrel, count out biscuits made of coarse flour, and carry food for the seamen from the galley to the forecastle, where they ate.

John soon learned that basically four classes of sailors were aboard ship: the captain and his officers, the able-bodied seamen who had been at sea for three years or longer, ordinary seamen who had been at sea for less than a year, and the cabin boy. John was at the bottom of the pecking order.

Once the voyage was under way, the bosun introduced John to some basic sailing skills, "learning the ropes," he called it. John had to learn the names of the sails, ropes, and lines and how each needed to be adjusted for different weather and sea conditions. To pull on the wrong rope in a storm could jeopardize the ship.

As they sailed down the eastern North Atlantic Ocean, John was surprised to discover that his father held a church service each Sunday on the ship's foredeck. He soon learned that the spiritual oversight of the crew was one of the captain's responsibilities. Although most of the sailors aboard scoffed at God, the Sunday services reminded John of the many promises he'd made to God over the years, both before and after his mother's death. So far out at sea and without a single friend, John renewed his pledge to be a good Christian. He decided he would pray each day, read his Bible before bed, and recite his favorite Isaac Watts hymns to himself as he drifted off to sleep.

John soon discovered that being a practicing Christian aboard ship was difficult. It was as if there were two armies warring inside him. One army wanted him to follow the path his mother had set for him in his early childhood, the way of prayer and piety. The other army lured him toward the coarsest sailors who drank and swore and cursed God at every opportunity. It was a constant struggle as both sides took turns battling each other for John's soul.

The ship's initial destination was northern Spain, where the vessel's cargo of corn was unloaded. It then continued sailing down the European coast, mooring in Portugal before passing through the Strait of Gibraltar and into the Mediterranean Sea. The weather was warm, and after Portugal, the weekly allotment of beer was traded out for Madeira wine, which kept longer in the hotter climate. Once in the Mediterranean, the ship sailed on to Italy, where it was loaded with a cargo of silk, dried fruit, and soap.

Like most of Captain Newton's other voyages, the ship was away at sea for nine months before returning to England. By the time it sailed back up the Thames River, it was spring. After furling the sails and dropping anchor, John and his father were rowed ashore in the ship's longboat and were soon reunited with Thomasina and her father. Much to John's surprise, his stepmother had given birth to a baby boy while they were away at sea. The baby was named William, but as John looked at him, it was hard for him to imagine the baby was his half brother. And it became even harder for him when John realized how much everyone else, even his father, doted on the boy. John's heart grew bitter watching his father embrace his new son and take an interest in his crawling and babbling. These were things John was sure Captain Newton had never done with him.

On his next voyage, John's father decided not to take John along. John wondered why, but he dared not ask him directly.

After Captain Newton left, John slipped back into the farm routine. Once again there wasn't enough work to keep him busy all day. So when he had finished his chores, he went back to hanging about with other local boys. By now they were all old enough to get into trouble. One day they vandalized an abandoned mansion, and another time John and his new friends shot a deer on the grounds of the local squire. John knew that poaching was a serious crime, punishable by either hanging or seven years' banishment to work in an American colony. John was relieved that the gamekeeper let them go after a sound whipping.

Not long afterward, John was riding his step-grandfather's horse down a lane when the animal reared and threw him off. The hawthorn hedge bordering the lane had recently been pruned. Just inches from where John's head landed, a thorny, pruned hawthorn stick poked out of the ground. After catching his breath, John stared at the stick and realized that had he landed three more inches to the left, the stick could well have poked out his eyes and possibly killed him. Back on his feet, John rounded up the horse and climbed back on. He rode home in silence thinking how in the past few days he could easily have been blinded or killed or transported to an American colony to work as retribution for poaching.

The words of various sermons John had heard over the years flooded his mind. Yes, life could be short, but eternity would last forever. He remembered his mother talking about Judgment Day. As the horse clopped along, John gave himself a stern lecture and determined to do better. As he'd done on the ship at sea, John rededicated his life to following God. He found his mother's religious books and read them—at least for a while. But once more the lure of friends and adventure won out, and he went back to his old ways.

John's father returned from his nine months at sea, though his return didn't mean much to John. However, when he left to return to his ship for the next voyage, he took John with him. Once more John would serve as cabin boy. The voyage followed the same route as John's previous one. Once again they kept a good lookout for pirates as they transported a load of wool to southern Europe, eventually returning to England with a cargo of silk, crockery, and spices.

When he returned to Aveley in spring 1738, John was approaching thirteen years of age and was eager to be reunited with his friends. He soon learned that a three-masted warship was anchored at Long Reach, on the Thames. The ship was being outfitted to sail to the West Indies to stop the Spanish from interfering with British ships in the Caribbean. John dreamed of sneaking aboard the vessel to impress his friends with how much he knew about ships. To make his dream a reality, he walked two miles to the Purfleet Jetty on the Thames, where he found a waterman who knew his father. John asked the man to row him and several friends out to the warship to look around it. The waterman agreed, and it was soon arranged that they would meet at one o'clock. on the following Sunday. John could hardly wait to tell his friends about the outing he had arranged for them.

Sunday came, and as usual John was required to sit with the family for their midday dinner. However, John's stepgrandfather took much longer than usual to eat the roast beef and suet pudding piled on his plate. There was no way John could leave the table until all the adults had finished eating, and as the minutes passed waiting for them to finish, he grew more anxious.

Once the adults had eaten, John was free to go. He ran most of the way along the marsh track to the jetty, where he had arranged to meet his friends. But when he got there, no one was waiting for him. As he looked out over the river, he could see two of his friends sitting in a skiff being rowed by the waterman. John was angry that they hadn't waited for him, and he yelled curses at them. Then, as he watched, the skiff hit a floating log and flipped over. It happened in an instant. Arms and legs flailed in the water. Yells were heard from nearby ships, but it seemed to take forever before another boat came alongside and pulled several people from the river.

John stood transfixed by a combination of fascination and horror as the rescue boat drew closer to the Purfleet Jetty. His two friends were lying in the bottom of the boat, motionless. The waterman was bent over them.

When the rescue boat reached the jetty and tied up, John learned the awful truth—both his friends had drowned. He was speechless. If his stepgrandfather had not taken so long to chew his meat, he too would have been in the skiff. And like his two friends, he could not swim. John shook uncontrollably as he helped lift the two bodies from the boat onto the jetty.

Attending his friends' funerals several days later, John was still in shock. He was haunted by the fact that he'd been so close to being with them in the skiff—and that *he* had organized the outing. He wondered if his friends were now in heaven or hell, and if he'd died, where would he be spending eternity? These sobering thoughts sent John back to studying his Bible and praying.

Soon after the death of John's friends, Captain Newton took John with him on a third voyage around the Mediterranean. This time John was not the cabin boy. Instead he signed on as an ordinary seaman and was sent down below deck to live with the seasoned sailors. As he'd done so many times before, John soon joined the sailors in cursing and carousing, and any thought of living a godly life quickly evaporated. By the time the ship returned to England, John was fourteen years old. Upon arrival home, his stepmother, Thomasina, announced she was expecting another baby.

John was not excited to hear about another baby, nor was he excited about going back to sea. He could read and write and knew some Latin, but not enough to secure a teaching job or work as a private tutor. And he didn't look forward to a future at sea aboard ships, where everything to him seemed dull and repetitive. He wondered how he might go about finding something more interesting to do with his life.

Apparently, his father had been thinking about the same thing for his son. In spring 1740, not long before John's fifteenth birthday, his father announced he'd found a new job for his son. He had signed John up to learn how to be a ship's merchant—in Spain. Within a month, John once more was aboard his father's ship, this time as a passenger. He was off-loaded from the ship at the port of Alicante, on Spain's southeastern Mediterranean coast. John went to study with an old friend of his father's to learn all there was to know about being a ship's merchant.

For John, things in Alicante were a disaster from the start. He had no interest in bills of lading or regulations on the packing and taxation of cargo. And while it would have been difficult enough for him to follow along and learn all of this in English, it was nearly impossible for him to figure out in Spanish what he was supposed to do.

When Captain Newton docked his ship at Alicante eighteen months later to check on his son's progress, John and his mentor both agreed that it was time for John to go home. John imagined his father would be furious with him. Instead he seemed resigned, as if he'd not really expected him to rise to the occasion. John didn't know which was worse, his father's anger or his indifference.

Father and son were back in Aveley by late autumn 1741, where John met his new half brother, Harry, for the first time.

A year and another voyage later, in November 1742, Captain Newton explained to seventeen-year-old John that he was taking a new job with the Royal African Company, which imported ivory and gold from Africa. He and Thomasina, along with William and Harry, would be moving into an elegant townhouse in London, but there was no room there for John. According to his father, it was time for John to strike out and make his own way in the world. This was astonishing enough to John, but there was more. Captain Newton had been in contact with Joseph Manesty, one of his friends in Liverpool who owned some ships and several prosperous sugar plantations in Jamaica, the wealthiest of the American colonies. Joseph had offered John the position of slave overseer on a Jamaican plantation with the opportunity of his becoming a planter before he was thirty years old. John jumped at the opportunity. He imagined being a planter in such a far-off place would be challenging, but he also knew that the rewards would be great. In twenty years or so, he could retire to England a wealthy man.

Soon everything was settled. John's father outfitted him with suitable clothes and fashionable luggage. By the end of November, John's bags were packed. John was eager to be on his way to Liverpool to board the ship that would take him to Jamaica.

To fill in the last two weeks before John left, his father asked him to undertake a thirty-mile horseback ride south to Maidstone, Kent, to deliver some legal papers. A hard winter had set in, and John was not enthusiastic about venturing out in it, but because his father had just spent a lot of money on him, he agreed to go.

On the day before John set out for Maidstone, he received a letter from his mother's distant cousin, Elizabeth Catlett. This surprised John, since he'd lost touch with her when his father remarried. Elizabeth invited him to visit her family anytime he found himself near their home in Chatham, Kent. She promised John that he would always receive a warm welcome.

While John had heard of Chatham, he had never been there. The town was located just over the Rochester Bridge on the Medway River, ten miles away from Maidstone and directly en route. *What a coincidence,* he thought. He would be going right past the Catlett house. Should he stop in and see Elizabeth? The last time he'd seen her she was helping his mother into the hackney carriage for the trip to Kent to recuperate. Did he really want to stir up all those painful memories?

Chapter 4

# Impressed

On December 12, 1742, John was on his way home from Maidstone. He was eager to get home before making his way to Liverpool and the ship that would take him to Jamaica and a new life. The vessel was due to depart at the end of the month. As he reached Chatham, heavy snow began falling, and night was not far off. John guided his horse from the main highway and rode a half mile along a lane. Soon he was standing at the front door to the Catletts' house. He had tied his horse to a hitching post, stomped his riding boots to dislodge the snow, and taken one hand out of its glove. Before leaving home, he'd received permission from his father to visit the Catletts for up to three days. John hadn't intended to stop, but the heavy snow had made him change his mind about riding straight home. He could do with a hot meal and a warm bed.

Standing at the Catletts' door, John hesitated. Was visiting a distant relative a mistake? He hadn't knocked yet. It wasn't too late to leave. He could turn around, climb back on his horse, and be on his way. He had no idea what awaited him on the other side of the door. But the cold and his curiosity got the better of him. John knocked on the door. A girl, about four years younger than he, opened it. She seemed surprised that anyone would be out in such terrible weather. "I'm John Newton," John stammered. "I've come to see Mrs. Elizabeth Catlett."

A woman came up behind the girl, gave John a puzzled look, and said, "Bless my soul. It's you, John Newton!" With that she rushed to him and enveloped him in a hug.

John stood, not knowing quite what to do. He hadn't been hugged since he was a young boy.

When Elizabeth at last let John go, she invited him to come in. "You must be freezing," she said. "We have a blazing fire waiting for you." She turned her head and called, "Jack, come here and get his horse in the stable."

John smiled. As he stepped through the front door, a young boy brushed past him and headed for his horse. "Thank you," John said, remembering to be on his best behavior.

"And this is my daughter Polly," Elizabeth continued as she helped John out of his riding cloak. John nodded at the girl who had opened the front door.

Soon John was sitting in front of the fireplace, surrounded by four children, three of whom just stared at him. They were his distant cousins, and they knew much more about him than he knew about them. John soon learned that Polly, at thirteen, was the oldest. Then there was Betsy, who was twelve, and Jack, eleven. Baby George was asleep in the cradle by the hearth. "And this is George," Elizabeth said, introducing her husband, who sat in a scuffed leather chair.

As the afternoon progressed, John learned more about his long-lost cousins. The oldest three attended school. Elizabeth and George Catlett believed that it was important for their children, even the girls, to learn to read and write. Jack loved reading Latin and didn't want to follow in his father's steps as a tide surveyor. George Catlett and John discovered they had a lot in common. As a tide surveyor, George was employed by HM Customs to board incoming ships and check their cargos against their bills of lading to see if they were smuggling goods into England without paying the appropriate taxes. George asked John many questions about his time at sea. The children listened attentively as John wove stories of storms endured and the colorful sailors he'd met on his voyages.

As darkness descended and the snow continued to fall, the Catlett family ate a meal of mutton stew and dumplings. John had never tasted anything so good.

That night, John shared a bed with Jack. Even though Elizabeth had placed a bed warmer between the blankets, John felt chilled lying there counting the days until he sailed for Jamaica. He recalled how some of the sailors he'd met at sea had told him it was even warmer and more beautiful in the Caribbean than the Mediterranean. John hoped so.

Yet while he thought about his future, John felt a strange twinge of regret about leaving. It was something he hadn't felt until a few hours ago, and he was sure it had something to do with stopping to visit the Catletts. Perhaps he shouldn't have come. They were all too nice, too welcoming, too much a family. *That's it,* John thought to himself. He had never spent a day with a real family before—parents and brothers and sisters who had grown up together and cared about each other. John thought of his half brothers, William and Harry, and how his stepmother, Thomasina, treated them so differently than she did him. It was hard to imagine their ever becoming a loving and caring family like the Catletts.

There was something else too—Polly. Although she was just thirteen years old, John was shocked to realize that he thought of her as more than just a younger, distant cousin. He noticed the way she giggled and how she had put her hand on his arm to invite him to the dinner table. Could he be attracted to her? John was seventeen, four years older than Polly, and about to embark upon a five-year-long contract in Jamaica. Although girls Polly's age were sometimes betrothed to be married, the idea seemed ridiculous to John.

John at last drifted off to sleep. He awoke the next morning ready to spend another day with Polly and the Catletts. He had spent time aboard ships with hardened sailors, but John tried to leave all thoughts of that life behind as he played games with the children. After lunch, the snow stopped, and they went outside in search of a suitable Yule log and boughs of holly and ivy to decorate the house for Christmas.

One day went by and then another. John knew he should be on his way again, but he kept putting off telling the Catletts that this would have to be a brief visit, that he had to be in Liverpool in a few days to catch a ship to Jamaica. He tried not to think about it at all, which was especially easy when he was with Polly. More days went by, and the Catlett family seemed delighted to think John might stay with them through New Year.

John knew he needed to leave. If he didn't, the ship would sail from Liverpool without him, and his father would be furious. In fact, John had no doubt his father would be anxious to know where he was right now—he should have been home several days ago.

Nonetheless, John stayed on with the Catletts in Chatham. He passed the days drinking wassail and engaging in friendly whist competitions with the neighbors. John and Polly would play as partners, and John was delighted to note that Polly was a sharp card player. He added this to the list of other charms he'd noticed about her.

On Christmas Day John went to church with the Catlett family. During the service, they sang Isaac Watts's popular hymn: "Joy to the world! The Lord is come." Singing the hymn took John back to the times he had attended church with his mother. He wondered how different his life might have been had she lived. Perhaps he would be studying at Saint Andrew's University in Scotland by now.

After three weeks of staying at the Catletts' home, John knew he had to pull himself away and go face his father. It was snowing again as he mounted his horse and rode away. He crossed the Rochester Bridge and arrived home late in the afternoon. At first John's father was relieved that he was alive, but his relief soon turned to anger. Of course, the ship for Jamaica had sailed without John. Captain Newton berated his son for embarrassing him in front of his friend Joseph Manesty and for throwing away the opportunity of a lifetime.

As punishment, Captain Newton signed John on as a crew member of a ship headed for Venice. John resigned himself, accepted his punishment, and joined the ship as it prepared to sail for the Mediterranean. This was the first time he'd been a sailor on a ship of which his father wasn't captain. He soon discovered how different it was without his father aboard. The sailors were more brutal and crude than he remembered. The ship made stops at ports around the eastern end of the Mediterranean before heading to Venice. As he worked aboard the ship, John thought constantly about Polly. He wondered if he had any hope that she might agree to marry him one day. He knew he would need much better career prospects if he were ever going to get Polly's father's permission to do so.

John survived the eleven-month voyage around the Mediterranean, arriving back in London in early December 1743. By now his family was living in the townhouse in London, and in February 1744, John accompanied his father, stepmother, and two half brothers to Aveley for a visit. While there, Captain Newton allowed John to ride on to Chatham to visit the Catletts. Once again, upon his arrival, John was embraced by the Catlett family. And John was delighted to once again be in the company of Polly. Yet his heart was in turmoil. He wanted desperately to tell Polly his true feelings for her but knew it was unwise to do so at present.

On March 1, 1744, John strolled along the waterfront of the Medway River as it wound past Chatham. He watched boats being loaded and unloaded as he wrestled with his feelings for Polly. As he walked, lost in thought, he failed to notice two men walk up beside him. Suddenly they linked their arms in his. Startled, John turned to see he'd been captured by a Royal Navy press-gang. The Royal Navy had legal right to capture and impress able-bodied British subjects to serve on their ships in times of war. And with a war looming between Britain and France, the navy was rounding up young men to fully man their ships should fighting break out. John, who knew there could be a war, suddenly realized how foolhardy he'd been in taking a stroll along the waterfront, especially since a naval base was located near Chatham.

Following his capture, John was taken to a local inn and locked in a room while the press-gang rounded up more hapless young men. While he waited, John managed to bribe one of his captors to hire a courier to carry a note he'd written to his father explaining his circumstance.

Two days later, John was relieved to hear Captain Newton's voice in the next room talking to the lieutenant in charge of the press-gang. John couldn't hear everything being said, but he hoped his father could secure his release. At last the door swung open and his father walked in. He looked angry as he explained to John that there was nothing he could do. The French fleet had amassed off Dunkirk on the north coast of France and had already fired on some British ships. Although war had not yet been declared, given the situation, John's father explained that the navy was not willing to release John, especially since he was already an experienced sailor. John's spirit flagged as his father said goodbye and left.

The next day, John and the nine other young men who had been rounded up by the press-gang were marched from the inn, loaded onto a tender, and taken out to the HMS *Harwick,* lying at anchor near the mouth of the Medway River.

The *Harwick,* which was 140 feet long and 40 feet wide, carried fifty cannons. The vessel had a crew of three hundred. Once he had been transferred aboard and taken below deck, John learned that many of the crew were criminals who had been sentenced to ship life instead of prison. Below deck, Captain Philip Carteret, commander of the *Harwick,* interviewed the new "recruits." When he learned that John had sailing experience and had served on the crew of ships on the Mediterranean trade, he gave him the rank of able seaman, while all those being impressed into the navy with him had the lowly rank of ordinary seaman. John was thankful for the higher rank.

On March 8, the *Harwick* set sail. For the next month, the newly impressed recruits were put through their paces learning the various tasks they were expected to do in both fair and foul weather. They were constantly climbing the rigging, sometimes in howling gales, where they practiced furling and unfurling the sails. They scrubbed the decks, learned to haul in using the capstan, and adjusted to the way the ship vibrated when her cannons were fired during training exercises. The firing of the cannons was new to John, but he was familiar with most of the other tasks aboard ship. What he wasn't so familiar with was the pace at which these duties were expected to be carried out. The bosun carried a cane with him on deck and would use it to beat any man he thought wasn't doing his job fast enough. John experienced several beatings as he learned to do things faster than he ever thought possible. At night, he crawled into his hammock, which was strung up in the overcrowded space that housed the seamen, who were located in the bottom of the ship below the waterline. The air was dank and stale, and the odor of so many men living in such close quarters was overpowering.

On April 3, 1744, John and the other members of the *Harwick*'s crew were paraded on deck, where they listened as Captain Carteret read aloud the formal declaration of war between France and Britain. Britain was now part of a broader conflict pitting several European countries and kingdoms against each other. Having entered the war, the British were aligned with the Habsburg Empire, the Dutch Republic, Saxony, Hanover, and Russia against France, Prussia, Spain, and their allies. John didn't understand all the details that had led to the war, and he knew he wasn't the only one aboard who didn't. Nonetheless, the *Harwick*'s crew were now supposed to fight to the death for their king and country.

Two days later, John was paraded on his own before Captain Carteret. Things usually didn't go well for those called before the captain. The men were often ordered to be flogged with a cat-o'-nine-tails for some infraction of the rules. John had no idea what he might have done that had brought him to the captain's notice. He needn't have worried, however. Captain Carteret had called John before him not to punish him but to promote him. John breathed a sigh of relief. The captain had learned that John's father was a respected captain with the Royal Africa Company and a man about whom he'd heard good reports. As a result, John was elevated to the rank of midshipman. The new rank meant that he was considered an officer in training and could move up to the quarterdeck to live and eat with the other officers.

John relished the new rank and living arrangement. As an able seaman housed in the gloom below deck, he'd been almost a slave. Now he was on his way to becoming an officer, a position that brought respect and, as John soon learned, more free time aboard.

Chapter 5

# Deserter

The *Harwick* joined a flotilla of Royal Navy warships escorting convoys of merchant ships to Scotland and Norway. In autumn 1744 off the Yorkshire coast, HMS *Harwick* encountered a French warship, the *Solide.* Once the masthead lookout reported seeing the billowing sail of the French ship, Captain Carteret barked out orders to give chase. John and the other crew members sprang into action, unfurling more sails, adjusting course, tightening lines, and preparing the cannons. After two hours of sailing, the *Harwick* caught up to the *Solide*. The captain gave the order to open fire. John felt the *Harwick* vibrate beneath him as gunpowder exploded and cannonballs shot out of the cannons. He watched as many of the cannonballs smashed holes into the side of the *Solide*.

The French returned fire at the *Harwick,* but somehow their cannonballs didn't inflict the same damage. Several just bounced off the *Harwick*'s hull. Once they had sailed by the *Solide,* Captain Carteret ordered the *Harwick* to come about so they could give the *Solide* another broadside of cannon fire. Before they had time to come about, the French ship struck her colors in surrender. The *Harwick* had won the battle. Captain Carteret dispatched longboats to take control of the *Solide.* Soon Captain Sourbert was brought aboard the *Harwick,* where he surrendered his sword to Philip Carteret as a cheer went up from the *Harwick*'s crew.

As the *Harwick* rejoined the convoy it was escorting to Scotland, John had to admit that of all his ship voyages, this was the most exhilarating one he'd experienced. The feeling of power that pulsed through the ship as the cannons fired had amazed him.

During December 1744, the *Harwick* lay at anchor between Deal, on the Kent coast, and the Goodwin Sands, a sheltering sandbank a few miles offshore. Rumor aboard ship was that early in the new year they would be joining several other Royal Navy vessels to escort a convoy of merchant ships to the Mediterranean. They were expected to be away from England for a year.

As the *Harwick* rocked at anchor, John's thoughts were on Polly Catlett. How could he go a year without seeing her? He could not bear the thought. He had to see Polly again. The town of Chatham lay about forty miles northwest of where the *Harwick* was anchored.

John asked Captain Carteret if he could go ashore for a visit. He was given permission to leave the ship for the day of December 20 but needed to be back aboard within twenty-four hours of leaving.

Early in the morning John was rowed ashore at Deal. He went straight to the livery stable, hired a horse, and set out for Chatham at full gallop. But no matter how fast he rode, John realized his trip was going to take him more than a day, at least if he wanted to spend time with Polly.

In mid-afternoon, he pulled the horse to a halt in front of the Catlett home. He thought his heart would burst when he knocked on the door and Polly answered it. Right then and there he wanted to confess his love for her and his hope she would marry him one day, but he knew the time wasn't right. He promised himself he would do it before he returned to the *Harwick*.

John knew he could stay no more than three hours in Chatham if he was to make it back to the ship on time. But as on previous visits, being with the Catletts caused him to forget about time and obligations. Before he knew it, he was sitting down to dinner with the family, and then he decided to stay the night, and the next day and the next night, until it was Christmas. By then John would be in deep trouble with Captain Carteret upon his return to the *Harwick,* but he still couldn't seem to tear himself away.

At last John plucked up the courage to tell Polly of his true feelings for her. He had expected her to say she felt the same toward him, but fifteen-year-old

Polly was less enthusiastic. And when Polly's father learned of John's feelings toward his daughter, he forbade John from visiting the Catlett home again. Meanwhile, Polly's mother took John aside and told him kindly but firmly that although Polly was approaching the age of marriage, John had few prospects to offer Polly as a husband. After all, he was an impressed crew member on a Royal Navy ship. Elizabeth said that Polly and John should go their separate ways and forget about each other. She also forbade John to write to Polly. John was cheered up though when Polly arranged to exchange letters with him through the auspices of an elderly aunt who lived close by. John would send his letters to the aunt, and she would see that Polly got them without her parents knowing and would send Polly's letters on to John.

Soon afterward, John set out to return to the *Harwick*. He arrived back at the ship on January 1, 1745. He was relieved to have finally expressed to Polly his love for her, and although things hadn't gone as he'd hoped, he was glad that he would still be able to pour his heart out to her through letters.

Captain Carteret was red-faced with anger as John stood before him on the deck. John had committed a huge breach of navy protocol by not returning on time, an infringement punishable by a whipping. However, some of the officers interceded with the captain on John's behalf, pointing out that he was smitten with love for a certain local girl and had not been thinking straight. Their words seemed to soften

Captain Carteret's anger. The captain gave John a verbal dressing-down for breaking the rules, but he did not order him flogged. John was thankful for that, but he knew that he had let the captain down and that the captain would probably never fully trust him again.

Once back on the *Harwick*, John learned there had been a change of plan. They weren't headed for the Mediterranean but rather would be helping to escort a convoy of ships around the Cape of Good Hope at the bottom of Africa and across the Indian Ocean to distant India. The ship would be gone from England for up to five years. The news devastated John. He'd been wondering how he would make it through a year away in the Mediterranean without seeing Polly, but not seeing her for five years was too much. She could very well be married off to some other man by then. Yet it seemed that John could do nothing about it. He wrote a long letter to Polly. "The first day I saw you I began to love you. The thoughts of one day meriting you (and believe nothing less could have done it) roused me from a dull insensible melancholy I had contracted and pushed me into the world," he began the letter.

Throughout January the *Harwick* lay at anchor off Deal as a squadron of navy and merchant ships assembled. The merchant vessels consisted of Indiamen and Guinea ships. The Guinea ships would be escorted to the west coast of Africa, and from there the *Harwick* and several other Royal Navy ships would travel with the Indiamen to India. At the beginning of February, the assembled squadron sailed down the English Channel and anchored off Spithead near Portsmouth. On February 23, 1745, under the command of Commodore George Pocock, the squadron set sail. As the *Harwick* unfurled her sails, John wondered how long it would be before he set foot in England again. He hoped Polly would await his return.

For three days they sailed westward. Then the wind turned to blow from the southwest, forcing the squadron to seek shelter in Torbay on the Devon coast. No sooner had the ships made it to Torbay than the wind changed again. Commodore Pocock ordered the squadron back to sea. They had gone only fifteen miles when the wind turned fierce, causing several of the merchant and navy vessels to run aground at Start Point.

Despite the grounded ships, Commodore Pocock kept the squadron headed toward the southwest. But as night descended on February 28, the ships rounded Lizard Point on the south coast of Cornwall into the jaws of a howling gale. In the pitch-dark, with the ships of the squadron bunched together, the crew of the *Harwick* worked furiously as Captain Carteret barked out orders. They were attempting to maneuver their ship through the gale while avoiding crashing into the other ships. Over the howl of the wind, John heard the crunch of several ships colliding, accompanied by yells and screams from the darkness. Fortunately, the *Harwick* was not caught in any collisions. At daybreak, the squadron limped back to land and dropped anchor in Plymouth Sound, where repairs to the ships got under way.

Throughout March 1745 the ships lay at anchor off Plymouth. As the crew of the *Harwick* worked away putting their ship back in order, hardly a day went by that John didn't think about Polly. During this time, several impressed sailors from the *Harwick* and other navy ships used the opportunity to make it to shore and desert.

Toward the end of the month, John learned that his father was at Torquay, twenty-eight miles to the east. John's father was organizing the repair of several ships belonging to the Royal Africa Company. John began to scheme. If only he could get to his father, he reasoned, his father would be able to find a way to exchange John's service on the *Harwick* for service on one of the Royal Africa Company ships plying the Africa trade. That way, John would be back in England far sooner than if he stayed on the *Harwick* all the way to India. Most likely he would be back home in about a year and able to see Polly again. The more John thought about it, the more he liked the idea.

On April 2, Captain Carteret ordered John to take a longboat and group of men ashore to collect fresh vegetables, drinking water, and other supplies waiting for them on the quay in Plymouth. By now, eleven men had deserted the *Harwick,* and the captain ordered John to watch the men carefully lest any try to escape.

After the longboat was rowed ashore and tied up at the quay, John ordered the men to start loading the stores into the boat. As he stood quayside supervising, John suddenly realized that this was his chance.

There would be no better moment to slip away and find his father in Torquay. With the men absorbed in loading the longboat, John slipped up the alley leading away from the quay. He walked as fast as he could, not wanting to bring attention to himself in case someone gave the alarm that he was deserting from the navy.

John walked eastward from Plymouth toward Dartmouth, beyond which lay Torquay. Night fell and he walked on before finding a place to sleep in a pasture. In the morning, he continued his walk. John estimated he was about two miles from Dartmouth when he noticed a group of marines heading toward him. Before he knew it, it was too late to avoid them. The marines spotted him and he had nowhere to run. One of the marines questioned John as to where he'd come from and where he was headed. John tried to make up a story, but it was obvious that they didn't believe it. John was arrested and marched back to Plymouth along with several other deserters the marines had rounded up.

In Plymouth John was locked up in prison while his fate was decided. Death was the usual penalty meted out for deserting the Royal Navy, especially during wartime. If Captain Carteret ordered him court-martialed, John knew he would be hanged. His future rested on the captain's decision. After two days waiting in jail, John was put in irons, rowed to the *Harwick*, and locked up below deck to await punishment. Captain Carteret decided not to court-martial him. Instead John would be flogged for his infraction.

Relief and dread pulsed through John—relief that he wouldn't be hanged and dread at the thought of the cat-o'-nine-tails lashing across his back.

A short while later, John was marched up on deck, where the entire crew was mustered to one side. On the other side, a grating had been set up. John's irons were removed. Then Captain Carteret walked out on deck. He ordered John to strip off his shirt and then had the master-at-arms tie John's hands and feet to the grating. A bosun's mate then stepped forward holding a cat-o'-nine-tails. The captain reminded everyone why John was being punished and ordered the bosun's mate, "Give him the first dozen." A drummer started a drumroll, and the bosun's mate raised the whip and brought it down hard across John's back.

Stinging pain surged through John as the cat-o'-nine-tails continued to lash across his back in rhythm with the drumroll. John felt blood running down his back. After twelve lashes, John was barely conscious. His back throbbed, and he was thankful for the respite when the drum stopped and the bosun's mate stepped back. A fresh bosun's mate then came forward to take up the whip. Once he was in position, Captain Carteret gave the order for John to receive the second dozen lashes. The drumroll started again, and another twelve lashes were applied.

After receiving twenty-four lashes with the cat-o'-nine-tails, John heard the order that was music to his ears. "Pipe down," the captain commanded. The flogging was over. John was untied from the grating, a cloth was placed over his pulsating, lacerated back, and he was carried below deck.

It was several days before the throbbing in John's back eased and the lacerations began to heal. By then the second part of his punishment had kicked in. John was stripped of his rank and made a lowly seaman. And now that he was healing, he was ordered back up on deck to work. The crew was preparing to get under way, and since John was no longer a junior officer, the other officers ordered him around. That was humiliating enough, but John had been an unpopular officer with the men below deck. Sometimes he had been unnecessarily cruel to them, just for the fun of seeing how they would react. Now that he was one of them, sleeping, eating, and working with those he had made miserable, things did not go well for him. Day and night, on deck or in their quarters in the bowels of the *Harwick,* the seamen made a point of paying John back for his actions. John seethed with indignation over the way they treated him.

On April 9, 1745, the *Harwick* and the other ships in the squadron departed Plymouth for Madeira. As they sailed past Lizard Point and left England behind, John felt a deep sense of loss. He wondered if he would ever see Polly again. And even if she waited for him, how long would it be until he returned home?

Chapter 6

# Plantain Island

The ship took eighteen days to sail the fourteen hundred miles from Plymouth to Madeira, the Portuguese Island that sat in the Atlantic Ocean, 550 miles southwest of Portugal and 400 miles off the coast of Morocco. In Madeira, HMS *Harwick* lay at anchor off the town of Funchal, where routine repairs and maintenance were carried out before the vessel sailed down the coast of Africa, around the Cape of Good Hope, and on across the Indian Ocean. The *Harwick* and several other Royal Navy ships would escort a convoy of merchant ships to India, where, once their cargo was unloaded, they would be reloaded with silk, tea, perfume, and opium for the return voyage to England. These were expensive items that French naval vessels and privateers loved to get their hands on, not to mention the sturdy ships carrying them.

Funchal was busy as ships came and went, picking up cargos of sugarcane and casks of Madeira wine and depositing slaves from the west coast of Africa to work on the island's various plantations.

John was heartily sick of life in the Royal Navy, especially now that he was considered the lowest-ranked seaman aboard the *Harwick*. For several days now he had been kept busy tarring the outer seams of the ship's hull. It was backbreaking, dirty work, using brushes to layer on hot tar. Before that, John had been in the bottom of the hold restacking provisions after they shifted during a storm. He'd also spent time high above in the rigging checking the ropes and lines. But no matter what he did, John knew he couldn't ease up on how fast he worked. Everyone aboard seemed to be watching him. If he slackened his pace for a moment, someone would report him and he would feel the bosun's cane swipe across his back. The only thing that seemed to keep him focused and moving forward was the hope that one day he would again see Polly.

On the morning of May 9, 1745, a month after setting sail from Plymouth, John was so exhausted he slept through the bosun's dawn whistle. Even the sound of his crewmates shuffling out of their hammocks hadn't awakened him. Suddenly John felt his hammock jerk. He fell to the deck and landed with a thud. "It's all you deserve, you lazy swine!" the bosun snarled with a curse as he sheathed his knife. In an instant John realized what had happened: the bosun had cut the rope attaching his hammock to the hull.

John felt a searing pain in his shoulder. With his teeth firmly clenched, he stood up, stowed his hammock, and climbed the ladder up to the main deck. He squinted in the bright sunlight as he emerged from below. All around tenders were plying the water carrying sacks of grain, crates of provisions, barrels of freshwater, and casks of Madeira wine out to the anchored British ships.

As he looked around, John noticed one of the other seamen from the lower deck standing at the side of the ship. The man carried a canvas bag, which he slung over the gunwale and then promptly followed it. John walked over to see what was happening. By then the sailor had climbed down a rope ladder and was standing in a tender at the side of the *Harwick*.

"I'm on my way," the sailor called up with a grin.

"What do you mean? Where are you going?" John yelled back.

"Been traded out to a Guineaman," the sailor replied.

John spun around. "Is that true?" he asked an officer standing nearby.

"Aye," the officer nodded. "The captain impressed two able seamen off the *Pegasus,* and he's doing the courtesy of sending them two of ours to replace them."

John's heart sank at the news. If only he'd been up earlier, he might have been one of the two seamen being transferred from the *Harwick* to the *Pegasus*. "So, who's the other one being transferred?" he asked.

"Not sure the captain's decided," came the reply.

John felt a surge of optimism. Perhaps this was his chance! He raced to find Captain Carteret. John knew that none of the officers or the captain liked him. Perhaps that was a good thing right now. Perhaps they disliked him enough to send him on his way to the *Pegasus.*

As it turned out, Philip Carteret appeared happy for the opportunity to be rid of John Newton. Ten minutes later John held his official discharge papers from the British navy as he climbed over the side of the ship and down the rope ladder into the tender. He had served aboard His Majesty's ship for one year and two months.

It was hard for John to believe that an hour ago he'd been asleep in his hammock on the *Harwick* and was now a crew member aboard a merchant ship on her way to the west coast of Africa. With any luck, in less than a year the ship should have completed her triangle trade voyage between the west coast of Africa, the Caribbean islands or the coast of North America, and back to England. John could hardly believe the turn of events.

Aboard the *Pegasus,* John was introduced to Captain Guy Penrose. He soon discovered that the captain knew his father and was prepared to give him a fresh start, signing John onto the crew as a petty officer. For the first time in a long time, John felt that luck was with him.

The *Pegasus* carried a cargo of cutlery from Sheffield, wool, and guns. When she reached the Windward Coast, the most westerly stretch of Africa, the ship would head south. Sailing down the coast they would stop at various trading posts, or factories as they were usually known, where slaves would be imprisoned in a structure called a barracoon. The British goods the *Pegasus* carried would be bartered for slaves. A healthy, young male could be had for ten pounds of goods along the Windward Coast and then sold for fifty pounds in the colonies across the Atlantic Ocean. Once the ship had collected a worthwhile cargo of slaves, the crew would make the fastest possible crossing of the Atlantic. This was known as the Middle Passage. When the ship reached the Caribbean, the slaves who survived the journey would be sold in Jamaica or Barbados. The ship would then be reloaded with sugar and rum for the return voyage to Britain.

As they sailed away from Madeira and headed for Africa, John busied himself with his shipboard duties. Sometimes when working down in the ship's hold, he would eye the equipment being carried in preparation for taking slaves aboard: nets, chains, ankle and wrist irons, and piles of wooden grating. Once on the coast, the ship's carpenter would use the wooden grating to fashion shelflike arrangements for the slaves to sleep on.

On July 24, 1745, as the *Pegasus* sailed south, John turned twenty years old. He didn't tell anyone it was his birthday, but he wondered if his father thought of him that day.

While delighted to be out of the Royal Navy, John quickly forgot the lessons he learned aboard the *Harwick*. Once more he acted arrogantly toward other crew members, was lazy, often ignored direct orders, and made fun of the captain and first mate behind their backs. While John showed little respect for most members of the *Pegasus*'s crew, there was one man aboard he did respect: Amos Clow. Amos was an Englishman and a resident trader, which meant he bought slaves from African merchants and locked them up in a series of barracoons he owned along the Windward Coast. He then sold the slaves at profit to men like Captain Penrose who sailed the Middle Passage and resold the slaves for profit.

Amos explained to John that most of the slaves in his factories were purchased from African chiefs and kings. Most of these slaves were taken prisoner during intertribal conflicts. Many of them had been marched a thousand miles or more from inland to the coast to be sold to resident traders. According to Amos, few Englishmen ventured far inland in Africa. It was too dangerous. As a result, little was known about life in the continent's interior. Amos also told John how he'd been born in poverty and arrived on Africa's Windward Coast with nothing. But by being willing to risk his life when going ashore and by working hard, he had risen to be a wealthy businessman. In fact, he was part owner of the *Pegasus*.

John listened enthusiastically to all Amos told him. Dreams of riches filled his thoughts. And as they approached the Windward Coast, Amos explained to John exactly how things would work for the next few months. The ship would sail up and down the coast trading for and taking aboard African men, women, and children, usually in groups of five or ten at a time. The male slaves would be shackled in irons and kept below deck. And since they often outnumbered the crew aboard by up to twenty to one, the sailors would be careful not to have too many male slaves above deck at the same time because they were constantly looking for ways to escape or commit suicide.

The slaves, both male and female, paid a high price if they resisted. According to Amos, they were whipped or beaten and sometimes thrown overboard as an example to others. John took in all the information. It seemed like hard work to him to keep a cargo of slaves alive and subdued, but Amos's wealth proved that the profit from such effort was well worth it.

On New Year's Day 1746, the *Pegasus* was anchored at the mouth of the Sherbro River when Captain Penrose suddenly took ill and died within hours. First mate Josiah Blunt took over as captain, while Captain Penrose's body was taken ashore for burial. John realized he was in trouble. His behavior aboard ship had made an enemy of Josiah Blunt—now Captain Blunt—whom John had lampooned in the various ditties he taught to the crew. John knew that when the *Pegasus* reached the Caribbean the new captain would delight in trading him back onto the first British navy ship they encountered. John didn't want to go through that ordeal again. Rather than risk such an outcome, he decided to throw in his lot with Amos and leave the *Pegasus* behind. Two days after Captain Penrose's death, John and Amos disembarked the ship in the Benanoes Islands.

John stood by the water's edge and watched as the *Pegasus,* running with the wind, sailed away from the islands. The ship soon disappeared below the horizon, and John was glad to know she was gone. He was eager to begin the next phase of his life as a resident trader. He liked the idea of going into business with Amos Clow. With any luck, he would be able to return to England rich enough to sweep Polly off her feet.

Amos had explained to John that the river mouths were strategic places to build factories. Most slaves were captured inland and ultimately arrived at the coast in canoes that took them down the rivers. Amos explained that there was a river mouth a short distance to the south that did not have a factory situated near it. He had a shallop stowed nearby, and the two men retrieved it and sailed twenty miles to the southeast down the coast to Plantain Island. The island was just south of the mouth of the Kagboro River and about two miles out to sea. The small island was about two miles in circumference, uninhabited, and named after Captain John Plantain, the infamous Jamaican pirate who once sought refuge there. Amos had previously leased half of the island. He told John it was the perfect spot for a barracoon and factory.

At first things went well. Amos owned slaves farther up the Windward Coast, and he brought them down to Plantain Island to build houses, slave huts, and a barracoon. Hundreds of coconut palms grew on the island, and some were cut down to make the huts, with the palm fronds forming their thatched roofs. The walls of a barracoon had to be sturdy enough to stop slaves from trying to escape and so were made of stones with mortar between them. The top of the wall was rimmed with glass from broken bottles.

When the buildings were finished, Amos left John on the island and made another trip one hundred miles up the coast in his shallop. When he returned, he brought with him an African woman named Pey Ey, whom he introduced to John as his wife. As far as John could make out, Pey Ey was the daughter of a tribal chief and had used her influence to help Amos buy his first batch of slaves at a good price, thereby setting him on the path to wealth. Pey Ey was a tall, strong woman who spoke a little English and seemed to take an instant dislike to John. He wasn't sure whether it was because she thought he might double-cross her husband or was jealous of the time the two men spent together planning. Whatever the reason, John knew he had a powerful enemy in Pey Ey. He was thankful to have his own coconut tree log house, and he tried to stay as far away from her as possible.

Once the barracoon was completed, John and Amos planned a two-month trading trip along the coast to buy slaves. But that all changed when John came down with a fever. He grew weak and was unable to keep food down. He knew the coast of Africa was called "the white man's grave," and he doubted he would survive his illness. Indeed, his bones ached so much he hoped he would die.

Since Amos couldn't delay the trading trip, he sailed off, leaving John in the fateful hands of Pey Ey. No sooner had the shallop been pushed off from the shore than Pey Ey ordered John to be carried from his comfortable house to an empty hut, where he was laid on a woven mat on the floor and offered nothing but a coconut log for a pillow. John wondered what he was in for.

Chapter 7

# Enslaved

John's body burned with fever. His mouth was dry and his lips were cracked. No one brought him water. He slipped in and out of consciousness. And in those moments when he was conscious, all John could think about was that his death was near. Yet he didn't die. Slowly the fever left him, though not before taking a toll on his body. He was so weak from pain and hunger he could barely stand up. All he wanted was food and water, but neither was brought to him. John wondered if he had survived the fever only to die of starvation.

Eventually a house servant brought John a few spoons of rice, which Pey Ey had said he could have. John ate it, but it did nothing to put an end to the hunger gnawing at his stomach. Another day passed, and then the servant brought a plate to John, telling him it contained the scraps from Pey Ey's dinner, which she was generously offering to him. John looked at the plate, which contained a spoonful of rice, half-chewed pieces of gristle, and vegetable scraps. John took the plate and ate the food. Back home in England he had fed scraps like that to pigs, but right now he was thankful for any food.

For many days—he didn't know how long—John lay on the mat in the hut and waited for someone to bring him food and water. One night Pey Ey ordered him to come to the main house. John mustered his strength and stumbled to the main house. "You can't sit down in my presence," Pey Ey told him. John wobbled on his feet in front of her, ogling the dishes of food set on the dinner table: mounds of rice, beans, a fruit platter. But none of it was for him. Instead, Pey Ey handed him a china plate containing her scraps. The plate was too heavy for John, and it tumbled from his hand to the floor and shattered. Pey Ey yelled at his clumsiness and ordered him to return to his hut with nothing.

On another night, John could stand the hunger no longer. He stumbled into the field behind the row of slave huts and fell to the ground. He pulled up roots, which he ate raw. They tasted terrible, but his hunger drove him to keep going, and slowly the gnawing pangs in his stomach began to subside. After he had eaten, he vomited everything up as he tried to get back on his feet.

Back in his cabin, John lay down once more. As he lay there he was surprised to note that even though he had vomited up the roots, his hunger had subsided, at least for a few hours. The next night he stumbled back to the field and ate more roots, which he again vomited up. And he did the same the next night.

Even though the slaves had a deep dislike for Englishmen, they began to take pity on John. After dark, some of them, shackled together in leg irons, would sneak into his hut and share some of their water and food rations with him. John was thankful to them, and as he ate, it occurred to him that he, an Englishman, was worse off than the slaves who lived on the island!

When Amos returned, John looked more like a walking skeleton than a man, but he was still alive. At the first opportunity, he told Amos all that had happened while he was gone and begged him to keep Pey Ey away from him. Amos didn't believe him. Instead, he took Pey Ey's side in the matter, telling him he believed his wife's story that she knew that John was trying to double-cross him and so she had taken matters into her own hands as a way to punish him.

As John's health and strength slowly returned, he could tell that Amos was now deeply suspicious of him. But the next time Amos left Plantain Island in his shallop on a trading trip, he took John with him. John was grateful. He never wanted to be left behind on the island with Pey Ey again. Besides, he saw the trading trip as an opportunity to earn back Amos's trust. But things didn't go quite the way John had hoped.

The two men traveled up the coast, stopping along the way to trade with the locals and at various factories. John worked hard and proved himself to be an able trader. He and Amos worked well as a team, and John felt he had won back Amos's trust. However, he was working on the shallop late one afternoon sorting and stowing away goods they had traded when Amos returned to the boat in a rage. He had been ashore drinking with a local trader, and he began cursing John and calling him a thief and cheat. According to Amos, the trader had told him that John was not to be trusted, that he was trying to deceive him, and that he was stealing food when Amos wasn't around. John protested his innocence, assuring Amos he wasn't cheating him and had never stolen anything from him. But once again Amos wouldn't believe him. And no matter how much John pleaded his innocence, he could not change his partner's mind.

John was banished from the main cabin of the shallop and left to sleep on deck that night. And in the morning, when Amos left to go trading, he chained John up with a long ankle chain locked to the railing of the boat. He left a pint of water and a cup of boiled rice as his ration for the day. After Amos and two of his slaves departed, John sank onto the deck. The African sun beat down on him. He was dressed in a thin cotton shirt and tattered cotton pants and wore a handkerchief knotted at each corner on his head for shade. He could hardly believe what was happening to him. But there he was, a prisoner once again, only this time chained up on deck.

Amos and the two slaves returned to the shallop after dark. Amos said nothing as he disappeared into the cabin below deck. Soon John smelled chicken being roasted on the brazier in the cabin. His mouth watered and his stomach rumbled. He was delighted when one of the slaves emerged from the cabin with a plate and told John the master wanted him to have some food. But his heart sank when he looked at the plate. On it was a scoop of boiled rice, a raw, unplucked chicken wing, and a pile of raw entrails. John wanted to retch. He knew he would vomit it straight up again if he ate it. But he couldn't waste it either. John used the uncooked chicken for bait to try to catch fish. He waited until the tide turned when the fish would be running, attached a piece of chicken intestine to a line, and dropped the line overboard. His patience was rewarded a half hour later when he pulled in a fish. He tore it apart with his fingers and ate it raw. Afterward, he stretched out on the deck to sleep.

The next day and the day after that, John was left alone chained up on deck in the sun. When they sailed to a new location in the shallop to trade, he was allowed to sleep below deck in the slave quarters. Once they arrived at their new location, John was again chained up on deck during the day. By now the rainy season was approaching, and heavy rain showers pelted down on him. After the showers passed, John would sit on deck shivering uncontrollably. The breezes that whipped across the surface of the water made it feel like his clothes were woven from ice.

On one occasion John was left chained up on the boat for two days and nights while Amos and his slaves went off trading ashore. While they were gone, a huge storm blew in. Thunder crashed all around and bolts of lightning lit up the dark clouds overhead. Then a tornado blew through. John was terrified. The water in the bay was whipped into a frenzy, and John feared for his life. He was sure that either the shallop would capsize and he would be drowned or the tornado would tear him from the deck. He balled himself up against the gunwale and waited for the inevitable, but both he and the shallop survived the tornado. John continued spending most of his time chained on deck and catching fish to keep from starving.

When Amos and John and the slaves arrived back at Plantain Island, John expected to be released from his captivity. But a worse fate awaited him. Amos marched him to the blacksmith's shop, where John was fitted with leg irons. From now on, Amos explained, John would be one of his slaves. He would live in a slave hut and each day would work the fields with the other slaves. If he didn't work hard, the overseer would be instructed to whip him.

Day after day, John toiled in the heat, weeding and tending a grove of recently planted lime trees. The work was backbreaking. Every day, amazed local Africans came to watch a white man work like a slave. John felt humiliated and alone.

By now John had given up any dream of making a fortune as a resident trader. All his energy went into staying alive. He rarely thought of Polly. He doubted he would ever be a freeman again, able to return to England and see her. Besides, he doubted she would even be interested in him after all he had been through.

As the days passed, John decided his only chance of being free again was to get a message to his father to come rescue him. He begged one of Pey Ey's house servants to smuggle some paper, a quill, and some ink to him. When John received them, he wrote a letter home. The servant risked severe punishment by placing the letter in Amos's outgoing mailbag just before it was taken aboard a departing ship. In all John secretly wrote three letters home. He knew the chances of any of them reaching his father were slim, but he clung to his only hope of rescue from the hell he was in.

The rainy season ended, and John had not been rescued. In fact, by then he'd given up all hope of his circumstances ever changing. He imagined his body being buried in a shallow grave on the island. The only time he managed to distract himself from his wretched state of affairs was when he studied his Euclidean geometry book. It was the one book he'd brought with him all the way from England. Late in the afternoon, when his work was done, John would drag himself down to the beach and write out geometry formulas in the sand with a long stick. Page by page John learned how to calculate angles and prove theorems.

John was sure that being able to escape into the world of concise mathematics was the only thing that kept him sane. However, in December 1746 John's situation changed overnight. A new slave trader arrived and set up a barracoon at the other end of Plantain Island. John surmised that the new trader must have started asking Amos some awkward questions about his "white slave," because not long after the new man's arrival, Amos unshackled John and told him the other trader wanted him.

John did not stop to ask questions. He ran to the other end of the island. Sure enough, the new trader had a large meal waiting for him. For the first time in over a year, John sat at a table and ate with a fork. It felt wonderful.

While John ate, the trader told him he had a factory about a hundred miles down the coast in the Kittam District on the southern branch of the Sherbro River. He asked John if he would like to help run the factory. John jumped at the chance to get as far away from Amos and Pey Ey as possible.

When he arrived at Kittam, John found a well-run trading operation that dealt in slaves, gold, and African carvings and arts. John finally felt like this was the life he was born to live. There was plenty of good food to eat and rum to drink. Before long he was making short forays inland, bartering and learning about the local cultures. As he traveled, the ideas of right and wrong he had learned back in England began to seem foreign to him. He accepted that twin babies should be killed because they contained evil spirits and that when a chief died, his wife and slaves should be buried with him. John knew that the sea captains who anchored offshore to trade laughed and said he had gone native, but he didn't care. He had no intention of ever returning to England. His new life suited him perfectly.

On a warm day in February 1747, as twenty-one-year-old John was preparing to travel inland to meet with a tribal chief and trade, one of the other white men who helped run the factory arrived at his door. With him was Captain Swanwick of the *Greyhound,* a merchant ship that had spotted the trading post's smoke signals and dropped anchor offshore.

"I'm told you are John Newton," the captain said.

"That I am," John replied.

"Then I'm glad to meet you. I've searched up and down the Guinea coast for you, but nobody seemed to know where I might find you."

"And what might you want with me that you have searched so long and hard?" John asked.

"My ship is owned by Joseph Manesty of Liverpool. He's a friend of your father's, I believe." John nodded. Joseph was also the man who had offered John a job as slave overseer on one of his plantations in Jamaica. "Well," the captain went on, "your father received your letter requesting help and asked Mr. Manesty if the next ship of his bound for the Windward Coast could find and rescue you. That ship was the *Greyhound,* of which I'm captain, and at long last I have found you."

"Indeed, sir," John said, staring at the captain. "But I hardly think I need to be rescued anymore, do you?" he asked sweeping his hand around the veranda of his house. "Once you get used to this, England seems a long way off . . . and very cold." He laughed.

Captain Swanwick did not join his laughter. "But your father said your letter was desperate. Don't you care that he is worried about you?"

"All fathers worry about their children, I have no doubt," John replied curtly. "I'm sorry your mission to reclaim me has not met with success. I don't have any intention of returning with you."

The captain looked puzzled and then, as if suddenly remembering something important, raised his hand and said, "Wait! I hate to confess this, but I had in my possession a large pouch of letters and papers that Mr. Manesty gave me. He said they were from your father and I was to take them to you. In my haste to set sail, I left them behind at my home, yet I remember one of the items your father said you would be pleased to receive."

John motioned the captain to sit down on a nearby chair on the porch. "What might that be?" he asked.

"It was a will, from a distant relative of your mother's, I believe," Captain Swanwick replied. "Apparently, she has left you an inheritance of four hundred pounds a year for life." The captain sat quietly for a moment and then added, "Yes, I am sure that was the amount."

Now John took notice. This was something he had not expected. An annual income of four hundred pounds was a substantial inheritance. He imagined it was from one of his mother's great aunts whom he had heard about but never met. And suddenly he thought of Polly Catlett. Such a large inheritance would surely sway Polly's father into letting him marry her.

"And of course," Captain Swanwick added, "you will be my guest on the voyage back. You'll dine with me. I have a few books on board you can read at your leisure."

"Now that's an offer I could accept!" John laughed, thinking of the hellish voyage out to the Windward Coast of Africa, first aboard the *Harwick* and then on the *Pegasus*. He could see himself lying on a bunk, reading and writing while the seamen toiled out on deck.

In an instant John made up his mind. "You have me!" he told the captain. "I believe it is time to return to England—and with an inheritance too!"

Within an hour, John had left Kittam behind and was being rowed out to the *Greyhound*. Like so many other pivotal events in his life, he had made up his mind on the spur of the moment, and now he would have to wait and see how things turned out for him.

Chapter 8

# "The Lord Have Mercy on Us"

The *Greyhound* had been plying the Windward Coast of Africa for five months. Once John was safely aboard, Captain Swanwick set sail for Cape Lopez, a thousand miles south down the coast, making stops at various trading posts as they went. The *Greyhound* wasn't a slave ship. Rather, she took aboard an exotic cargo of ivory, gold, sandalwood, and beeswax for transport back to England. Since the ship wasn't a slaver, she had a smaller crew of about twenty men.

At first John enjoyed the luxury of having nothing to do. As a guest of the captain he soon located all the books aboard and read through them one by one. He also spent time each day reviewing his Euclidean geometry. But as time passed, he became bored with geometry and books. He began drinking heavily with the crew and was soon blaspheming with the best of them. On occasion, Captain Swanwick reminded John to tone down his language. Parliament in London had recently passed the Profane Oaths Act, which forbade the use of profanity. John tried to keep his speech clean, but cursing quickly crept back in.

By the time the *Greyhound* reached Cape Lopez, almost on the equator, John was thoroughly sick of ship life, and they still had five months of sailing ahead of them before arriving home. The trip could have taken longer, except Captain Swanwick was determined to make the seven-thousand-mile voyage to England in one leg, without any stops. From Cape Lopez the *Greyhound* sailed to Annabona Island, 250 miles off the African coast. The ship took on all sorts of provisions, including kegs of freshwater and barrels of flour, sugar, grains, and other staples, as well as sheep, pigs, goats, and chickens. The animals were placed in hastily erected cages above deck. The chickens would provide eggs and the goats would provide milk on the trip. Throughout the voyage the animals would be slaughtered one at a time to provide meat for the crew. By now, because of the death of several crew members from accidents and disease, the ship's crew had shrunk from twenty to thirteen. As the *Greyhound* set sail from Annabona, she was seriously undermanned for the voyage ahead.

To get back to England, the ship would follow an indirect route that took advantage of the prevailing trade winds. It would follow a large arc westward across the Atlantic Ocean and then head up the coasts of South and then North America before crossing the North Atlantic eastbound to Ireland and on to England.

Since the *Greyhound* didn't carry a heavy load of slaves but had a relatively light cargo that included a lot of buoyant sandalwood and beeswax, the vessel made good time. It sailed westward across the Atlantic, sighting the far northeasterly point of Brazil before turning north. While they stopped at no ports, at times they sailed close enough to shore for John to make out hills and trees and occasionally buildings. Caribbean island mountains appeared above the horizon as they sailed northward and then up the North American coast. It wasn't until the *Greyhound* arrived in the Labrador Sea just south of the British North American colony of Newfoundland that Captain Swanwick ordered the sails furled and the anchor dropped.

The ship bobbed at anchor on the Grand Banks, the world's richest codfishing grounds, while John and the ship's crew fished. The men pulled in codfish after codfish, which were filleted, salted, and placed in storage barrels in the hold. The fish would be used to supplement their diet as they crossed the North Atlantic Ocean. After a day and a half fishing on the Grand Banks, on March 1, 1748, the captain gave the order for the anchor to be raised and the sails unfurled. Far off in the distance the coastline of Newfoundland disappeared over the horizon. It would be John's last glimpse of land until the *Greyhound* reached Ireland.

The weather was fair as they sailed away from North America, and John hoped it stayed that way. Like the captain and crew, he knew that the *Greyhound*'s state of repair was barely adequate for a calm crossing. The ship had endured a lot during its time in Africa. The tropical sun and saltwater had frayed many of the ropes and lines that held the sails taut, and the sails themselves were heavily patched. The heat had caused the hull planks above the waterline to shrink and split, allowing the oakum and tar that kept the joints watertight to fall out. In a heavy storm the ship could be in danger of taking on water and sinking. But John reminded himself it was March, and spring was the calmest season in the North Atlantic. And even if the vessel took on a little water during the voyage, her holds filled with buoyant sandalwood and beeswax would counteract its effect.

Heading out across the North Atlantic, John had run out of things to do. It never occurred to him to offer his services as a crew member. He preferred being the only guest aboard. He had read through almost all the books onboard except for a few religious volumes. In a fit of boredom, he picked up one of them, an English translation of a book titled *The Imitation of Christ*. The book was written by a German priest named Thomas à Kempis in the 1400s and was now considered a classic of literature.

John decided to read the book for its intellectual content, not its religious ideas. At first he was able to, but on March 9, eight days after setting off from the Grand Banks, John was struck with a terrible thought: What if the ideas in the book were true? Thomas à Kempis wrote, "True peace of heart can be found only by resisting the passions, not by yielding to them," and "Consider then how miserable thou makest thyself by placing thy confidence or thy joy in any other save the sweet Friendship and Company of Jesus." Such words made John nervous. They echoed back in his mind to the times he had sat on his mother's knee as she drilled him on Bible verses and sang hymns with him. He'd long since decided the Bible and the God it spoke of was a myth, but still something stirred in his heart as he read Thomas à Kempis's words.

Frustrated with the way *The Imitation of Christ* made him feel, John slammed the book shut and shoved it back onto the shelf in the captain's cabin. It was one book he wasn't going to finish, no matter how bored he got during the rest of the voyage. That night John went to bed determined to think no more about religion.

He was awakened in the early hours of the morning as his body slammed against the bulkhead. For a moment, John didn't know what had happened. Then the *Greyhound* lurched in the opposite direction, tossing him to the far side of his bunk. Then he heard a loud bang. Was it thunder, or was it a mast falling onto the deck? John wasn't sure. He lay on his bunk in the dark listening. He could hear water splashing with each roll of the ship. Soon he realized the noise of water was coming from inside the cabin. He put his arm over the edge of the bunk and felt cold water. At the exact same moment, he heard someone yell, "All hands on deck! We're sinking!"

As John jumped from his bunk and raced barefooted toward the ladder leading up onto the deck, he heard a sickening crunch. Something had breached the hull, John was sure of it. He jumped onto the bottom rung of the ladder and frantically began making his way up. He heard Captain Swanwick standing at the top yelling to him, "Get a knife!" John was reluctant to go back below—the ship could turn into his coffin at any moment—but he obeyed the captain. He jumped from the ladder. As he went in search of his knife, a crew member brushed past him on his way up to the deck. John found a knife and a coil of rope and climbed up on deck with the items. As he emerged through the hatch, the captain yelled, "Erskine's been swept overboard! Go man the pumps. And for goodness' sake, lash yourself down!"

Seaman Erskine was the crew member who had pushed past John on his way up to the deck. John realized that if he hadn't turned back to get the knife, he could well have been the one swept overboard. Now the already short-handed crew was down to twelve, and John knew their only hope of survival lay in his joining with them. He took his place at one of the bilge pumps with another sailor. Together they worked the pump, pulling the handle up and down, up and down. But there was so much water inside the ship that the pumps were not enough. Soon other sailors were using buckets and large pots from the galley to help bail out water.

By now the *Greyhound* was headed into the wind, water washing across her deck. The buoyant cargo helped the ship ride up and over the massive waves coming straight at her. But each wave stressed the damaged ship, and John wondered how long she could last. He had often imagined how he might die. Perhaps it would be from some tropical disease in Africa or from wounds he received in a brawl with another seaman. Now John was sure he knew. He was about to drown in the North Atlantic Ocean, gone with no trace. His father and Polly Catlett would never know exactly what had happened.

Still, it was not time to give up. John's back ached, and he shivered as icy cold ocean water sprayed over him, but he kept at it, up and down, up and down, as the pump spat water from inside the hull back into the ocean.

About ninety minutes after John was tossed awake in his cabin, dawn broke. The wind abated some, and for the first time John and the others aboard could see the full extent of the damage to the *Greyhound*. In some places the rotting hull planks above the waterline had splintered, leaving gaping holes that allowed water to pour in. The ship was in worse shape than John had imagined. Meanwhile, other crew members raced below and grabbed as much clothing and bedding as they could carry. They tore the fabric into strips, stuffing it into cracks between the hull planks before nailing the strips in place.

After nine hours of manning the pump, John didn't have the strength to go on. Every muscle and bone in his body ached, and he shook from the cold. He made his way below deck, collapsed onto a sodden bunk, and fell sound asleep. He was awakened an hour later and ordered to get back on deck. It was his turn to take the helm.

Captain Swanwick helped John lash himself down at the helm. As he turned to walk away, John blurted, "If this won't do . . . then the Lord have mercy on us." The captain turned and stared at John for a moment.

It was then that John realized what he'd said. He hadn't intended to utter those words. They just came out. Throughout his time on the *Greyhound,* John was the one who had blasphemed and used profane words the most. No wonder Captain Swanwick was startled by his statement.

As John manned the helm on through the afternoon, he wondered if reading *The Imitation of Christ* just hours before had caused him to call out to God. He was confused. Had he meant those words? Did a part of him believe in God, after all?

John remained at the helm for eleven hours, until midnight, when he was relieved and again crawled below deck. He slept until early the next morning. By now the storm had mostly abated, and the crew had pumped out most of the water. But as he looked around, John realized that a new ordeal was beginning. During the storm, the decks of the *Greyhound* had been swept clean. All the livestock and crates of food had gone overboard despite being lashed down. The news got worse. Captain Swanwick told John that all the remaining food for the crew below deck had been spoiled by seawater. All that was left were several barrels of dried peas intended to feed the pigs and a few barrels of salted codfish. It wasn't a lot to work with, though there was still plenty of freshwater in kegs in the bottom of the hold. The captain implored the crew to stay calm. Enough food remained to get them home. After all, they were getting close to the Irish coast.

Aside from their losing most of their food stores, their biggest cause for concern was the condition of the ship. She had a large hole in her side, and water still seeped inside through gaps in the planks. The men would have to nurse the vessel along, always keeping the damaged side to leeward. This was challenging in the best of conditions, but with one of the masts snapped and the rigging damaged, John knew it would be an almost impossible task. Yet they had no choice but to try. And to his surprise, John felt strangely calm about the situation he found himself in.

"Land ho!" John heard the first mate yell at daybreak on the fifth morning after the storm had subsided. As the sun rose, everyone crowded on deck to see the beautiful sight: an island on the horizon with high, rounded hills. "It must be Ireland," Captain Swanwick said. "Bring the rum."

The remaining twelve men aboard stood on deck and toasted their deliverance by draining the last of the rum in the captain's keg. They laughed and clapped each other on the back. "We're saved," the bosun said. "We'll be docked this time tomorrow."

As the sun continued to rise, the sky over the land in the distance turned brilliant red. Then, like a puff of wind, the land was gone. "Clouds and mist on the horizon—a mariner's mirage," the captain said. "Have faith, we can't be far from land. We still have plenty of water and a meager ration of cod. We won't starve."

The following day, John wasn't so sure that Captain Swanwick was right about that as one sailor working a pump keeled over and died from starvation. They buried his body at sea. To make matters worse, a stiff wind blew in and pushed them northward. The damaged, leaking ship had no way to fight the wind and stay on an easterly heading toward Ireland. They were at the mercy of the wind and sea, headed toward the frigid north. The crew huddled to stay warm and consumed their meager rations—no more than a mouthful of cod and a pint of freshwater. When he wasn't manning a pump or taking his turn at the helm, John was cold, hungry, and near exhaustion. He didn't know how much longer he or the ship could hold out.

After several days, the wind that had been driving them north began to turn east, pushing the *Greyhound* along with it. By now the ration of codfish was gone, and the men discovered that the precious freshwater had leaked out of the remaining barrels in the hold. As he dozed off to sleep that night, John was sure the end had come for them all.

As John slept a fitful sleep, hunger gnawing at his stomach, the ship's fate changed. Just after dawn John heard a sailor yell, "Land ho!" This time it was not a mirage. As they came closer, Captain Swanwick recognized the island of Tory off the coast of Donegal, Ireland. The ship sailed eastward as best it could past the island and then turned south. At midday on April 8, 1748, the *Greyhound,* with her punctured hull, broken mast, shredded sails, and starving crew, limped into the shelter of Lough Swilly on the northern coast of Ireland. She dropped anchor off Buncrana Castle. John and the surviving crew were put on longboats and rowed ashore.

It took almost two months to repair the *Greyhound*. During that time, John took a room in a lodging house in nearby Londonderry. Oddly, he felt an undeniable urge to go to church and read the Bible. He did both twice a day and spent many hours alone praying. He longed for someone to talk to about his spiritual condition, but he didn't know anyone who he thought would understand him.

John also had time to write to his father, who replied with interesting news. Captain Newton had been offered a post with the Hudson's Bay Company as commander of the York Factory on Hudson Bay in the far north of North America. John vaguely remembered that the place was situated in the Arctic Circle. In the letter, Captain Newton even offered John a position at the factory, which traded in animal furs, if John arrived back in England before he had to set sail. John's father also had family news. While

John had been away, his stepmother, Thomasina, had given birth to another child, a daughter whom they named Thomasina.

The newly repaired *Greyhound*, with John aboard, arrived back in Liverpool, England, at the end of May. Upon disembarking, John was handed another letter from his father. This letter informed him that his father had been unable to wait any longer before setting sail for Hudson Bay and he had departed the day before. John also learned that there was no inheritance awaiting him in England. Captain Swanwick had made up the inheritance story to lure him onto the *Greyhound* in Africa and take him safely to England.

Both pieces of news were bitter blows to John. His father had already left, and he had no one with whom to discuss his future. Also, he had none of the promised money with which he had planned to support himself and prove to Polly's parents that he was able to take care of their daughter if she married him.

Dejected, the only person John could think to talk to about his situation was Joseph Manesty, his father's old friend and the owner of the *Greyhound*. Although he hoped for the best, John didn't expect much from Joseph. After all, he had let the man down six years earlier when he failed to catch the ship to take him to Jamaica. And of course, he was certain that by now Captain Swanwick would have told Joseph how badly John behaved on the *Greyhound*. Would Joseph be able to look past John's behavior and help him? John hoped so.

Chapter 9

# First Mate

Joseph Manesty received John warmly in his office. "Welcome back," he said, shaking John's hand. "It's good to see you. Captain Swanwick has visited me and told me about your courage during the storm and afterward as the *Greyhound* limped toward Ireland. It's just as well they had a passenger like you aboard."

John smiled. He could hardly believe how complimentary Joseph was being. Then the conversation took another unexpected turn. "How would you like to captain one of my vessels? You've proved you have a steady hand and don't lose your head in an emergency."

"I don't know what to say," John replied, and for once he really was speechless.

"Think about it," Joseph said. "The *Brownlow* is currently being built in Liverpool specifically for the slave trade. I'd pay you five pounds a month for the year or so you'd be out at sea, along with a share of the profits from buying and selling the ship's cargo. I hear you've a good eye for buying slaves."

John was shocked by the offer. He had come to ask for a job and now was being offered a ship! "Thank you. I'll have to think it over," he replied. The words sounded strange to John as he said them. He wondered where they came from. In all his life he'd never told anyone he would think something over. He loved to make snap decisions and see where they led.

Joseph seemed to understand and invited John to stay with his family. John was grateful. Since his own father had already left for North America, he felt suddenly shy about seeing his stepfamily or Polly again.

John loved his time with the Manesty family in their country home. He hadn't realized how much he missed the English countryside, especially in spring. The meadows were thick with cowslips and crowfoot, and honeysuckle wound its way around the hedgerows. Robins and wrens darted in and out of the flowers, carrying straw in their beaks.

As he took in the beauty around him, John thought about his future. He didn't know how to be anything but a sailor, and if that was going to be his livelihood, he needed to think carefully about how to proceed. The extra money a captain earned appealed to him, but the job came with some perils. He would be the one responsible if the ship ran aground on a reef or it was intercepted by a privateer or, perhaps worst of all, the crew mutinied. The more John thought about such possibilities, the more nervous he felt about becoming a captain, at least right now. He decided a better course of action was to offer himself as first mate on the *Brownlow*. This would allow him more time to learn the leadership skills he would need before taking on the responsibility of captain. He talked the idea over with Joseph, who agreed it was a prudent course for John to follow.

Once he had settled on a plan for his immediate future, John caught a coach and headed south to visit his family. His stepmother, half brothers, William and Harry, and his new half sister had all stayed behind at the family's home in London when John's father left to take up his position with the Hudson's Bay Company.

Just before he left Liverpool, John had received a letter from Polly's aunt informing him that before his father departed for North America he had visited the Catlett home in Chatham. The result of the visit was that Polly's parents and John's father had agreed that John could ask for Polly's hand in marriage. It would be up to her whether she said yes or no. And the letter contained more good news: Polly and her family were presently staying in London.

John was astonished by the turn of events. He sat staring at the letter for a long time as the coach rattled south. His father had visited the Catletts and talked about John's wanting to marry Polly! It was almost too much to believe. For six years he had dreamed of marrying Polly, always imagining that the obstacle to their being together was her parents and his lack of good job prospects. Now, it seemed, the obstacle had been removed. Polly's parents were willing to take him as he was. But what about Polly? Now that he had permission to ask for her hand in marriage, what would she say? On the trip to London, John rehearsed what he would say when he asked Polly to marry him, until at last he had the words down pat.

Upon arrival in London, John went to see his stepmother and half siblings, and for once he was glad to see them all. He especially enjoyed watching his new half sister, Thomasina, toddling around the room. It made him realize just how long he'd been away.

After two days with his stepfamily, it was time for John to visit nineteen-year-old Polly and learn her answer to his marriage proposal. He set out the next morning on foot. As he got closer to the house where the Catlett family was staying, he began feeling queasy. By the time he reached their door, he felt so nervous he wanted to vomit. And despite having rehearsed many times what he would say to Polly, when he was at last alone with her he found himself tongue-tied and unable to get the words out. Instead of asking for Polly's hand in marriage, John asked if he could write to her when he got back to Liverpool. Polly agreed without much enthusiasm, and before he knew it, the visit was over.

To save money John walked the two hundred miles back to Liverpool. It took him eight days, and during those days, instead of dreaming about a future with Polly as his wife, he chastised himself for being too nervous to ask her to marry him when he had the opportunity.

Back at the Manesty home in Liverpool, John wrote to Polly, telling her how he really felt about her, though he was still too shy to directly ask her in the letter to marry him.

Polly replied quickly. She thanked John for his letter and wished him well on his new venture as first mate aboard the *Brownlow*. She also said she would like him to visit her again on his return to England. John was heartened by the tone of Polly's letter, especially the fact that she wanted him to visit her again. With a light heart, he set about helping to outfit the *Brownlow* for her maiden voyage.

In August 1748, the *Brownlow* was ready to sail from Liverpool. Captain Hardy had been the first mate on the *Greyhound*, and he and John got along well. Including the two of them, the *Brownlow* carried a crew of twenty-three men.

The voyage south to the Windward Coast of Africa took two months. When the *Brownlow* arrived at the mouth of the Sherbro River, John and Captain Hardy soon discovered it was a "bad season" for buying slaves. Fewer people were being captured inland and marched to the coast to be sold. This meant that they would have to pay more for each slave they acquired. It also meant that instead of the four months they had hoped to spend plying the coast purchasing their slave cargo, they would most likely have to spend twice that before their holds were full.

As was usually the practice aboard slaving ships, Captain Hardy sent his first mate (John) ashore along with a group of sailors to do the trading. Slowly, one by one the shore party collected slaves, who were transferred to the *Brownlow* and taken into the darkness below deck. The men were manacled and chained together in pairs at the wrist and ankles. They were then forced to lie on stacked wooden platforms with only three feet of headroom. The women and children, some with babies in their arms, were housed below deck in the stern of the ship. For sixteen hours a day, the men were forced to lie on the platforms below deck in darkness. They were brought up on deck to exercise in the early afternoon and to be fed a meager meal in the late afternoon before being pushed below deck again.

John and the rest of the crew carried rifles, and a cannon loaded with shot was trained on the deck, ready to halt any slave rebellion. Nets were placed around the deck so that slaves couldn't throw themselves overboard and try to escape or commit suicide.

Despite the misery around him, John believed that being first mate on a slave-trading ship was an honorable position. Almost no one in England objected to the treatment of the slaves, and he tried his best to treat them better than slaves on other ships. During the Middle Passage, John saw his role almost as that of an English jailer, except that his "criminals" were aboard a ship and it was his job to transport as many of them as possible safely across the Atlantic Ocean to the Caribbean. He realized that conditions for the slaves they carried were harsh, but the ship's owner had to make money, so it was necessary to pack as many slaves as tightly as possible aboard ship.

Conditions aboard the *Brownlow* were harsh for the crew as well. On average, one in five crew members who set sail from England on a slave trader died before the voyage was over. In January 1749, while they continued to sail up and down the Windward Coast trading for slaves, seven crew members caught a tropical disease and died.

By June 1749, the *Brownlow* had taken aboard nearly a full load of slaves. The ship anchored off a river mouth for several days, and in the afternoons John took the longboat and four crew members ashore to stock up on provisions before heading out across the Atlantic. The crew rowed the longboat a mile upriver where they gathered boatloads of wood to stoke the cooking fire aboard ship and collected freshwater for the voyage. Each night, John and the sailors slept on the riverbank beside the loaded longboat before heading back to the ship in the morning.

On the eighth and last day of gathering provisions, John was about to climb into the longboat when Captain Hardy called him back. "Don't you go today," he ordered. "The second mate can take your place."

"Do you want me to do something else?" John asked.

"No," the captain replied, "nothing in particular. Just let the second mate go."

John agreed, though he was puzzled as to why Captain Hardy didn't want him to go ashore.

The following morning a native canoe paddled up beside the *Brownlow*. It brought bad news. They had seen the *Brownlow*'s longboat sink and everyone aboard drown. John was speechless at the news. Captain Hardy's order, which seemed to John to have been given on a whim, had allowed him to escape death.

John was still in shock over the event when Captain Hardy ordered the *Brownlow*'s crew to unfurl her sails and set the compass heading westward. It was time for the Middle Passage. If all went well, in six to eight weeks they would be docked at the island of Antigua in the Caribbean.

On the voyage westward across the Atlantic, since John didn't have too much to do aboard, he turned his attention to learning Latin. He had brought some Latin texts with him, and he spent hours each day translating them. Although he'd had little schooling, John realized how much he loved studying languages. It was a strange hobby for a budding sea captain.

John knew that during the voyage no captain wanted to lose any of the slaves he had traded for, especially when slaves were in limited supply and the captain had been forced to pay higher prices than normal for them. Yet John also knew that slaves did die aboard ship, mostly from disease, particularly dysentery, given the close quarters they were forced to endure, often with vomit and feces smeared about. The *Brownlow* was no exception. As the vessel made her way across the Atlantic Ocean, 62 of the 218 slaves aboard died. While most deaths were from dysentery, four were killed by crew members while attempting to escape. Several others had managed to find a way to climb over the "safety" nets around the open deck and throw themselves and their young children into the ocean to drown. The bodies of the dead were thrown overboard, and sharks trailed the ship.

About a week from their arrival in Antigua, the *Brownlow*'s crew began preparing the slaves for arrival. The men were shaved and given haircuts. Their manacles were removed to allow inflamed and infected areas on their wrists and ankles to heal. Shortly before arriving, all the slaves were rubbed down with palm oil to make their skin glisten.

The *Brownlow* reached Antigua in mid-August 1749, a year after setting out from Liverpool. John and Captain Hardy hurried ashore to meet with Joseph Manesty's agent. The agent told them that the price of slaves had fallen in Antigua, and Joseph wanted them to sail on to South Carolina in hopes of getting a better price for them.

Once the ship docked in Charlestown, South Carolina, a thriving town with a population of about seven thousand, John's first job was to get the remaining 156 African men, women, and children unloaded from the *Brownlow*'s holds so they could be sent off to the slave markets to be sold at auction.

Following the off-loading of the slaves, the next job was to return the vessel to a fit condition to sail. The holds were now caked in vomit, blood, and excrement. The stench was overwhelming. The lowest-ranking sailors were sent below to scour the wood surfaces with sand and vinegar. It took two weeks of constant effort before the holds were ready to be loaded up with cotton, rice, and tobacco, which they would transport back to England to sell.

John had not totally forgotten his interest in Christianity that had been revived during the voyage home on the *Greyhound*. While docked in Charlestown, he passed the time walking and praying in the woods on the outskirts of town. He also sought out somewhere to go to church on Sundays. He attended the Independent Congregational Church, where the Reverend Josiah Smith preached. John was struck by Smith's life and message. Smith, the first man born in South Carolina to hold a degree, which he received from Harvard College, spoke about inviting George Whitefield to preach in his church. John had heard about Whitefield, who had ridden on horseback from New York to Georgia preaching to huge crowds about the love of God. Josiah Smith liked to preach on the same subject. In fact, his sermons stirred John, yet often they left him with more questions than answers. Before he had time to seek answers from the preacher, the time for the *Brownlow*'s departure from Charlestown for England had arrived.

Chapter 10

# Captain

The *Brownlow* sailed from South Carolina in late October 1749. Unlike John's previous perilous crossing of the Atlantic, this voyage was calm and uneventful. The ship sailed into the Mersey River and docked in Liverpool in mid-December. After being away for sixteen months, John was home at last. During the voyage, many of his thoughts and prayers had been directed toward marrying Polly. Now he wondered if he had the courage to ask her in person.

As soon as he could, John caught a coach to the Catlett home in Chatham. He wasn't sure he had the courage to propose to Polly, but after seven years of knowing her, he realized he had to do it. When he finally got the words out, again, Polly was less than enthusiastic. She confessed her worries about his reckless behavior and how he always seemed to be in trouble with the authorities. John assured her he had outgrown that phase of his life and was now a responsible young man. As proof he cited the fact that Joseph Manesty had offered him another ship to captain. Polly admitted that was something positive to consider, but John was determined to press her for a yes or no answer. Finally, she said yes.

John Newton and Polly Catlett were married at Saint Margaret's Parish Church in Rochester, Kent, on Wednesday, February 11, 1750. The small wedding was attended by just Polly's family.

Now that they were married, John got cold feet about returning to sea as captain. Not only would he be away from Polly for up to a year and a half at a time, but also he had a one-in-five chance of not returning at all. Desperate for an alternative, John looked around. The simplest solution he came up with was gambling. If he could just win some bets, he would not have to leave to go back to sea. But things didn't go well. John kept gambling to try to make up for the money he had lost. Eventually, he borrowed seventy pounds and used it all buying lottery tickets. After he had lost everything, John knew he needed to face reality. He had to go back to sea, and also he was now encumbered with a seventy-pound debt. Polly was not impressed. On August 1, 1750, John left Polly with her parents and made his way back to Liverpool. There his new ship, the *Duke of Argyle*, was ready to provision for the journey ahead. The vessel was a refitted 140-ton, three-masted scow, fast and agile in the open sea.

In his new role as captain, John signed the crew aboard. They consisted of a first and a second mate, a surgeon, a boatswain, a cooper, a gunner, a steward, a cook, a tailor, eleven able seamen, and nine ordinary seamen—a total crew of thirty men including John. The ship also had room for two hundred slaves aboard.

Captain John Newton set sail on the *Duke of Argyle* on August 14, 1750. He was sorry his father was in North America and not dockside to see him off. His father was in the last months of his three-year contract with the Hudson's Bay Company and would be back in England when John returned from the voyage. He looked forward to seeing John again, especially now that he was a grown man with a wife.

Before departing Liverpool, John bought a 450-page leather-bound journal in which he intended to write down the details of the voyage. On his first evening, he sat at the desk in the captain's cabin and by the light of an oil lamp wrote, "Praise be to God. Journal kept on board the Duke of Argyle, Scow from Liverpool to Africa. Commenced August 14, 1750." Following this John included a quote from Psalm 107:

> They that go down to the sea in ships, that do
> business in great waters;
> These see the works of the LORD, and his wonders in the deep.

Each day in the journal John listed his activities, what he had read in the Bible, his Latin translation work, the fitness of his crew, and the ship's bearings. He also recorded the carpenters' progress building partitions below deck to separate the male slaves from the women and children. The gunner installed a cannon on the main deck to aim at the slaves when they were above deck exercising.

John read his Bible each day and set up a rigorous daily schedule of prayer for himself. As captain, John was determined to influence the behavior of the sailors aboard. Although he'd once been as bad as any of them, he now felt that cursing, brawling, and drinking too much threatened the well-being of everyone aboard ship. On Sundays, he called the ship's crew together for prayer, and then at four o'clock in the afternoon they came together again for Scripture lessons. During this time, John read the most well-known Bible stories, such as Jonah and the great fish and Joseph and his many-colored coat, to the crew. Most crew members appeared to know nothing of them, and many said they had never heard a sermon preached in their lives.

John felt he had to do something about the situation. He wrote a letter to his old pastor, Dr. David Jennings, asking him to write a simple set of prayers and Bible stories for sailors, promising that he would buy the first one hundred copies and ask other captains to buy them for their crew members as well. The letter, along with the regular ones he wrote to

Polly, went into a bag that was transferred to the next homeward-bound ship they sailed past.

No one was more relieved than John when flotsam appeared around the ship and the seafoam turned brown with silt. They were near land. Sure enough, on October 23 the watch called out, "Land ho!" The *Duke of Argyle* had made it to the Windward Coast of Africa, off Sierra Leone.

Two days later, John ventured ashore to learn what the trading conditions were like this year. He soon discovered that Captain Ellis of the *Halifax* had been there before him and had already purchased the best of the slaves on offer. Worse yet, slaves everywhere were scarce, and the scarcity had driven the price for them even higher. John doubted he would be able to completely fill the holds of his ship with slaves as Joseph had ordered him to do. Nonetheless, that day John did buy three slaves, two men and a woman. He didn't give them names, he simply recorded them in the ship's log as "numbers one to three."

The *Duke of Argyle* spent the next several months sailing up and down the Windward Coast looking for healthy slaves to buy. At each stop they made, John or his first mate bargained and cajoled the native traders to sell them their best people. Slowly, slave by slave, John began to fill the holds of his ship.

On the voyage from England, the crew had been relatively compliant, but once they reached Africa, many of them became unruly. They began testing John in every way possible, including directly refusing to carry out his orders. John had some of the worst offenders chained and flogged. He wondered if their rebellion was triggered by the fact that as captain he was just twenty-five years old or because he insisted on religious activities aboard the ship.

One night several of the sailors "borrowed" the longboat from the *Duke of Argyle* to visit a French frigate anchored nearby. The crew members from the *Duke of Argyle* all got drunk and started a fight with their French hosts. Vastly outnumbered, they jumped back into the longboat and rowed away from the French ship, right into a rocky outcrop. The boat was stuck fast, and the men were too drunk to figure out how to get off the outcrop. The next morning John needed to go ashore to trade for slaves and discovered the longboat missing. When the crewmen rowed it back to the ship later in the day, John had all the men who had participated in the escapade stripped, tied over a barrel, and lashed with a cane until they were semiconscious. Afterward they were put in irons for three days.

Even this didn't cure the wayward crew members' behavior, however. When they reached their next destination, John had had enough. He instructed the first mate to look out for any British navy vessels in the area. If one was spotted, he was to raise a flag signifying they wanted to come alongside.

HMS *Surprise* was spotted at anchor in an estuary along the Sierra Leone coast. The *Duke of Argyle* came about and anchored beside HMS *Surprise*. John was rowed over to the navy vessel, where he was welcomed aboard by Captain Baird. The two captains drank some rum together and talked about their time in Africa. Then they got down to business. John told Captain Baird he had three men on his ship in need of some naval discipline. Captain Baird agreed to impress the three troublemakers if John would take aboard three men from HMS *Surprise* who had been impressed into service but turned out to be terrible sailors. A deal was struck, and John was glad to be free of the three worst troublemakers on his ship.

In late May 1751, the *Duke of Argyle* sailed away from Africa with two hundred slaves aboard. At first the vessel made good time as the wind filled her sails and propelled her forward. Sailing westward, John urged the crew to keep a close eye on their human cargo. However, they unfettered one male slave and allowed him up on deck to sit in the sun because he had developed a large ulcer on his leg. Somehow this man found a marlinspike and was able to pass it through a grate to the slaves chained below.

One sharp-eyed sailor noticed that the spike was missing, and a search for it began. As the sailors searched, a fierce storm began to blow in and engulf the ship. By the time the missing spike was found, twenty slaves had used it to pry off their fetters. By then the storm was raging, and in such conditions John knew his men couldn't recapture the slaves who had freed themselves. He ordered the crewmen back on deck and gave them orders to shoot and kill any slave who tried to escape.

All night the sailors watched over the hatch until in the morning the storm blew itself out. By early afternoon John was relieved to learn that all twenty slaves who had freed themselves had been recaptured and were back in fetters.

John had iron collars fitted to each man who had pried off his fetters. The collars fit snug around the men's necks and were wide enough so that one edge rubbed against the shoulders and the other edge against the jaw. The collars were not meant to be comfortable. That was the point. They were a punishment to those who had tried to escape and a deterrent to those who might try. John was aware that his life and the lives of the crew depended upon his exerting tough discipline aboard. If the slaves ceased being awed by his potential to harm them for trying to escape, there would certainly be a slave rebellion and all would be lost. For John, iron collars were a way to keep the slaves in awe of his power. He didn't want to do permanent physical damage to them, because that way they would be worth less at market.

On July 31, 1751, John stood on the deck of the *Duke of Argyle* watching the sun set over the hills of Antigua straight ahead. The eight-week Middle Passage from Africa was over. John listened as several female slaves burst into song at the sight of the island. He felt satisfied, since only six slaves had died during the voyage—an excellent record. In preparation for their arrival, the male slaves had all been shaved and fed extra food, and their skin had been oiled. They were ready to be paraded before potential buyers.

Although he had a vague idea of what lay ahead for the slaves he transported, John was still shocked when Joseph Manesty's representative came aboard the *Duke of Argyle* to talk business. "You know," he told John, "I've done calculations on the best method to manage the slaves. Some planters think we should have them do only a moderate amount of work so they don't run down physically. They want to preserve them so they can work for as long as possible, even into old age. Other planters believe they should strike while the iron's hot and get as much work out of the slaves as they can—wear them out until they become useless and die, and then buy fresh slaves to replace them. My skillful calculations indicate that smart planters should work their slaves until they drop dead from exhaustion and then get new ones. A plantation run that way is more profitable and will seldom own a slave who has managed to survive for eight or nine years."

Later that day, one of the crew retrieved a mailbag that had been delivered to a coffeehouse in Antigua to await the arrival of the *Duke of Argyle*. John was glad to see that the bag contained several letters from Polly. There was also one from his stepmother. That letter carried bad news. John's father was dead. He had drowned while swimming in the sea at Fort York on Hudson Bay. There was talk of a severe bout of cramps or perhaps a seizure, but no one was sure exactly what happened. The details didn't matter to John. Eight years had passed since he had last seen his father, and he'd been hoping that when they both got back to London a new chapter in their relationship would begin. But now those hopes were dashed.

At least John was thankful to have a friend aboard the *Duke of Argyle* with whom he could share his sorrow. The friend was the ship's surgeon Robert Arthur, with whom John had forged a close bond during the voyage.

The ship took five weeks to be repaired and prepared for her final leg of the triangle trade journey back to England, including having her holds loaded with a cargo of rum and sugar. Because they had spent longer than expected gathering slaves in Africa, the *Duke of Argyle* was completely off schedule. As a result, they would be crossing the Atlantic Ocean during the volatile second half of the hurricane season, something ship captains always tried to avoid.

Chapter 11

# Chains, Bolts, and Shackles

Despite it being hurricane season, the weather held, and the *Duke of Argyle* arrived back in Liverpool on October 8, 1751. Once the vessel was unloaded, John delivered the ship's log to Joseph Manesty and traveled south to Chatham to see his wife. Polly welcomed him back, and the two took long walks together as they caught up on their time apart.

During his time at home, John made several trips back to Liverpool to confer with Joseph and plan his next voyage. This time he would be in command of a brand-new ship, the *African*. Many details had to be taken care of, including buying extra canvas to stow aboard so the crew could repair their sails and procuring enough iron bars from South Wales to be used to buy slaves once they reached Africa.

For John, his time in Chatham with Polly passed too quickly, and in early July 1752 he set sail on his second voyage as a slave-ship captain. Three weeks into the voyage, he celebrated his twenty-seventh birthday. The trip south to Africa's Windward Coast was routine, and John had the first mate take responsibility for getting the ship there. During this leg of the trip, John spent his time praying and studying the Bible and his Latin texts.

The outbound voyage went well. The *African*'s first mate proved capable, and the crew were well enough behaved. But once they reached the coast of Africa and began the process of trading for slaves, things began to change. One crew member died suddenly, and another became seriously ill with dysentery. This sailor confessed to John that the crew were plotting a mutiny. They would throw him overboard, take control of the ship, and sail to a different port in the Caribbean where they would sell the slaves and keep the money. The sailor who had died was one of the main ringleaders of the mutiny, and since his death, the other ringleaders and crew members had begun to have second thoughts. With this revelation, John sprang into action. All captains feared mutiny, and when they learned of one, it had to be dealt with swiftly. John rounded up the other ringleaders and put them in irons as punishment and to set an example for the other crew members.

John also did something he'd never done before when confronted with issues related to his crew. Although he punished the ringleaders, he didn't point the finger of blame at the rest of his crew. Instead, he asked himself if he had been a good captain or if somehow he had provoked the plot against him. Writing in his journal he wondered if he had "by any harsh or unworthy carriage of mine to the people under my command provoked or driven them to this attempt. I hope I can sincerely say that I have from the first day of the voyage endeavored to do my duty to them without oppression, ill language, or abuse as remembering I also have a Master in Heaven."

Besides dealing with the crew, John dealt with many challenges on the Windward Coast trying to trade for enough slaves to transport to the Caribbean. After eight months of trading, the holds of the *African* were still not filled. John set course for the largest slave factory on the Sierra Leone coast on Bence Island in the estuary of the Rokel River and Port Loko Creek. This large trading factory was maintained partly by an annual grant of ten thousand pounds from Parliament in London. Sure enough, there were many strong, healthy slaves to choose from at Bence Island, and John bartered hard for them.

John got the extra slaves he needed to fill the *African*'s holds, and soon afterward he set sail back across the Atlantic Ocean. A week into the voyage, John regretted buying the slaves from Bence Island. These slaves were big and strong, and they all seemed to know each other. They also understood the same language and talked among themselves. John was sure they were plotting escape. Sure enough, after he had the crew search the holds, they found knives, stones, shot, and a chisel. The situation was serious. A month earlier the African coast had been buzzing with the news of another slave ship from Liverpool being in a similar situation. The slaves had rebelled, and before it was over, the first mate, four seamen, and nineteen slaves had been killed.

John couldn't let such a thing happen under his command. When he sighted a regular trading ship headed for the Caribbean and about to pass them in the Atlantic, he signaled the captain and went aboard. After some hard bargaining, he convinced the trading-ship captain to take aboard the six most troublesome slaves and deliver them to Saint Kitts, where the *African* was bound. After the six troublemakers were transferred from the *African,* the remaining slaves became docile, and John had no more difficulties with them during the rest of the voyage.

On June 24, the *African* reached Saint Kitts. John was delighted to find several letters from Polly awaiting him. Polly was a laborious letter writer and didn't write about the deep, theological topics of the day that John would have liked to read about. However, he was grateful to have a wife who cared about him while he was away at sea. He arranged a parcel of dried fruits and a fresh pineapple to be sent home to Polly on the first ship leaving Saint Kitts for England.

The 167 slaves the *African* transported across the Atlantic were sold for a good profit. John had plenty of time to spend his share ashore at coffeehouses as well as visit wealthy plantation owners in their homes. The plantation owners welcomed the British captains, who brought them the latest news of events in England and the west coast of Africa.

The *African* weighed anchor from Saint Kitts for Liverpool on July 11, carrying a cargo of rum and sugar. John was glad to be on his way again. It was much easier to be disciplined with his prayer and study at sea than on land.

The vessel reached Liverpool on August 30, 1753, after thirteen months of being away at sea. In Liverpool John rented a room and rode to Chatham to visit Polly and bring her back with him. Living in the rented room in Liverpool was the first time in their three years of marriage the two of them had lived apart from Polly's parents. John thoroughly enjoyed his life on land, and he began to wonder if the life of a slave-ship captain was for him. Although he had loved ships since he was a small boy, he wrote in his journal that he had never imagined his job would involve "chains, bolts, and shackles." He sometimes felt more like a prison guard than a captain, but the real question was, If he was not a captain, what else could he do? He loved to learn from books, but a self-taught man could not get very far in England. Had he been younger and richer, he would have gone to university and earned a degree, but that was not possible now. He knew he would have to stick with ships and sailing for a long time to come.

John tried to look on the bright side. Joseph Manesty offered him the opportunity to invest in his fleet of ships, and slaving provided good financial returns. In just twenty years, the number of slave ships sailing from Liverpool for Africa on the triangle trade had grown from fifteen to one hundred fifty. These ships carried half the total number of African slaves traded across the Atlantic, and the trade didn't look like it would be slowing down anytime soon.

Within six weeks of arriving home, the *African* was scrubbed and repaired and made ready for her next voyage. The vessel sailed again from Liverpool in mid-October 1753, with John as her captain once more. The voyage down to the coast of Africa was fast, and John arrived in good spirits. However, even fewer slaves were available to buy than there had been on the previous voyage.

Ten weeks after arriving in Africa, John wrote in his journal, "Met no encouragement in the slaving way though had several of the best traders on board and am well known to them all. But the ships that got the start on us have flooded them with goods so that I could not persuade them to take any." The price for a fit young man had gone from 70 iron bars to 120. No captain wanted to sail the Middle Passage with less than a full cargo, since he would have to explain to the ship's owners why he hadn't made enough profit on the voyage. After another three months, John felt he had to sail anyway. Some of the first slaves he had purchased on arrival had been down in the hold so long their condition was deteriorating.

Cutting his losses, John set out on his third crossing as captain of the Middle Passage. This crossing turned out to be his easiest thus far. The holds were not crammed as usual. They had only 87 slaves housed in them rather than the normal number, 220. As a result, the captive slaves had plenty of room to exercise. The *African* arrived in Saint Kitts on May 22, 1754. John was amazed that on the crossing not one single crew member or slave had died. He had never heard of such a thing.

In Saint Kitts John carried out the now familiar task of selling the slaves he had transported and arranging for the money from the sale to be transferred to England. Then it was time to get the ship cleaned, repaired, and restocked for the trip home. This took several weeks.

Normally John spent the time ashore waiting for his ship to be made ready by relaxing at hospitable plantations or in quayside coffee shops. But this time he met another English captain, named Alexander Clunie. John was drawn to Captain Clunie right away, and his ears pricked up when he heard him say something about praying. Could the man be a Christian too? John soon discovered he was, and he invited Alexander aboard the *African,* where they could talk privately.

Captain Clunie was the first captain John had met who was open about his faith. Within hours of meeting, the two men were inseparable. It turned out that Alexander had been a Christian for much longer than John and enjoyed talking about his faith and the Bible. What a relief it was to John to find someone who understood and with whom he could unburden his heart. The two men studied the Bible together, and Alexander encouraged John to pray aloud, something he'd always struggled to do. He also gave John the names of several Christian leaders whom he felt John should hear preach when he got back to England. Among them were the Reverend Samuel Brewer, pastor of the Stepney Dissenting Chapel in London, and John Wesley, founder of the Methodists.

Captain Clunie's ship sailed first from Saint Kitts, though the *African* departed not far behind, on June 20. The journey home across the Atlantic was by far the most pleasant John had experienced. He had a lot of time to think over the things Alexander had spoken about, and he looked forward to going to meetings led by the Christian leaders who had been recommended to him.

The *African* docked safely in Liverpool in early August 1754. As usual, John visited Joseph Manesty and handed over the ship's logs and other important papers. Although Joseph was not pleased with the smaller financial return from the voyage, he seemed pleased with John's performance as captain. In fact, he offered John the position of captain on another new slave ship being built at John Fisher's shipyard. The vessel would be ready to go to sea in six weeks. Joseph even invited John to name the ship.

Before returning to Chatham to see Polly, John visited the vessel, which he named *Bee*, at the shipyard. A month sped by, and John and Polly returned to Liverpool together for the final preparations before the *Bee*'s maiden voyage, taking a room in a boardinghouse near the docks.

It took longer than anticipated for work on the *Bee* to be completed. October and November came and went before the ship was finished and moored at the dock ready for her maiden voyage. The crew went aboard and made themselves at home. John stowed the books he planned to study on the voyage and watched as the ship's holds were filled with goods to trade for slaves on the African coast.

When he was satisfied with how things were progressing, John left the first mate to take care of the last-minute details while he went ashore to spend the last two days at the boardinghouse with Polly. John was looking forward to setting sail in a new ship he had named. But things did not work out the way he'd planned.

## Chapter 12

# Tide Surveyor

John picked up his teacup and looked over at Polly seated beside him in the boardinghouse parlor. It was hard to concentrate on what she was saying. His mind was already on the voyage ahead. Today was his last full day in England. Tomorrow, in command of the *Bee,* Joseph Manesty's newest ship, John would set out on his sixth voyage to Africa.

John took a sip of hot tea from his cup. As he set the cup down, severe pain passed behind his eyes. He felt dizzy. The room went out of focus. John felt himself slump forward. His world went black.

An hour later, John regained consciousness and found himself laid out on the parlor sofa. Polly was leaning over him, her face streaked with tears. The landlady and the scullery maid were also there.

"Thank God you're alive!" Polly sobbed, holding John's hand. "You're alive. I thought you were dead."

The landlady stepped forward. "How do you feel?" she asked.

John tried to form words, but they wouldn't come.

"Do you know who I am?" Polly asked.

John lifted his head an inch. More pain shot through his skull and settled behind his eyes. Once more his vision went blurry.

It was a day before John could sit up, two more days before he stood on his own, and a week before he was well enough to walk outside. By that time the *Bee* had sailed without him as her captain. The doctor explained to John that he'd had some kind of apoplectic fit, something that was likely to recur throughout his life. Furthermore, John would be a danger to himself and others aboard ship if he ever sailed again as captain or even as a deck officer. His seagoing days were over.

The news was a stunning blow to John. After the initial sting of the separation from Polly at the start of each voyage, he enjoyed the challenge of navigating a ship and crew halfway round the world and back again. But now that was behind him, and he had no idea what his future held.

When John was well enough, he and Polly packed their belongings and traveled back to Chatham to live with the Catletts. No sooner had the couple settled back into the family home in Chatham than Polly became seriously ill. The doctor couldn't say what she had but confided in John that it could be a nervous disease brought on by the stress of his sudden apoplectic fit. Whatever the cause, Polly's health became a major concern. She was so sick she moaned with pain whenever anyone walked across the floor of her bedroom. The noise and vibration were too much for her.

John tried his best to help his wife. One thing he could do for her was to pray. He would take long walks in the Kent countryside during which he begged God to heal Polly and help her find peace. The various doctors who came to visit Polly did what they could, and each warned John that Polly could die any day. Whatever happened, John determined to stick to his Christian faith through the ordeal. Whenever he could, he rode into London to meet with the Reverend Samuel Brewer, pastor of the Stepney Dissenting Chapel, whom Captain Alexander Clunie had told him so much about.

Samuel Brewer encouraged John to attend various meetings and experience as many different preaching styles as he could. John fell into a routine of spending six days helping take care of Polly and then setting out early on Sunday mornings to hear preaching anywhere from Fleet Street, London, to Maidstone, Kent. He often took in three church services a day.

On June 6, 1755, Samuel Brewer furnished John with a letter of introduction to George Whitefield, who would be preaching at several services in Moorfields Tabernacle in East London. Whitefield had recently returned to England following his fifth visit to the North American colonies. Because John knew of his reputation as a fiery preacher and was eager to meet the man, he visited him the next day. Whitefield was busy finishing some letters that had to be put on a ship for South Carolina by late afternoon and could give John only five minutes of his time. However, he gave John a ticket for the following morning's communion service at Moorfields Tabernacle.

On Sunday morning when John arrived for the service, he found the tabernacle packed with four thousand people. He showed his ticket for the service, took a seat, and waited for the service to begin. When the communion service finished over three hours later, John was dumbfounded by what he had experienced. In the course of the meeting, the congregation sang twenty hymns. John was impressed with the way Whitefield talked between them, linking each hymn to the other and to the gospel, encouraging, exhorting, and challenging the congregation all at the same time. The power of Whitefield's preaching left John awestruck. The man's sermons pulsed with energy. Other preachers seemed dull by comparison. In fact, John went back to hear Whitefield preach at Moorfields Tabernacle twice more that week. After each sermon he left feeling challenged and invigorated in his faith and deeply impressed with George Whitefield.

Throughout the time of his illness, and now Polly's struggle with a mystery disease, John depended on his meager savings and the hospitality of his in-laws to get by financially. But the situation couldn't last. John needed to find a job. Given his earlier apoplectic fit, he was confident that neither God nor his doctor wanted him back at sea. He was more convinced of this when he learned what had happened to Captain Potter, who had taken over command of the *Bee* when John became ill. Captain Potter, along with most of the crew, was killed aboard the *Bee* during a slave uprising.

At the end of June 1755, John received a letter from Joseph Manesty asking him if he would be interested in being the chief tide surveyor of Liverpool. If so, he was willing to approach Thomas Salusbury, a member of Parliament and the lord mayor of Liverpool, to see if he could secure the job for John. John was astonished. The position of tide surveyor was a prestigious one that required a wealthy and powerful patron to acquire.

John thanked Joseph for his interest in his future and said he would gladly take the job of tide surveyor of Liverpool if it was offered to him. *Who wouldn't?* John asked himself. The position paid a salary of 150 pounds a year, and as chief, he would be overseeing a staff of sixty men. The job required a tide surveyor to board every ship entering the Port of Liverpool and assess the taxes due on the vessel's cargo as well as look for any smuggled goods hidden away onboard. Not only would he have a steady government income, but also as a captain, John knew that tide surveyors in every port received "strokes"—special fees and gratuities paid by captains and ship owners above the customs duties assessed on their cargo. These strokes, or bribes, were meant to ensure that a captain would get "special consideration" from the tide surveyor if he needed it. John knew that these payments could sometimes add up to as much as his annual salary. All in all, the job sounded perfect for him, though he had little confidence he would beat out other applicants with stronger ties to their patrons.

To his surprise, a month later John received word that the job of the tide surveyor of Liverpool was his. He rode to Liverpool to meet with Joseph Manesty and thank him for his effort in helping to secure the job. Sitting in Joseph's office, John learned about the "coincidences" that led to his appointment as chief tide surveyor. Joseph had been tipped off that the current tide surveyor of Liverpool, Mr. Croxton, was about to resign. Joseph wrote to Thomas Salusbury recommending John for the soon-to-be vacant position. Thomas took Joseph's recommendation that John was well qualified to handle the job. He wrote to the secretary of state in London, recommending John for the position. That was when Joseph learned that he had been misinformed. Mr. Croxton had no intention of resigning his position as tide surveyor.

An embarrassed Joseph knew that he would have to write a letter of apology to Thomas Salusbury, who would then have to notify the secretary of state of the confusion. But to Joseph's utter amazement, Mr. Croxton died in his sleep that night. Now the job of the chief tide surveyor of Liverpool really was vacant. Several of Liverpool's politically powerful men moved quickly to secure the tide surveyor's job for a family member or friend through patronage, but it was too late. The decision had already been made in London. Following Thomas Salusbury's recommendation, John Newton had already been appointed the new tide surveyor of Liverpool.

John was astonished when he heard the story of how he came to get the job. He was about to turn thirty years old, and as far as he was concerned, getting the job was the best birthday present ever. He was convinced that being appointed tide surveyor was what he had been praying for. But to take up the job he would have to leave Polly with her family in Chatham, as she was still too sick to move. However, having received one blessing from God, John was determined to keep praying for a second one—Polly's full recovery.

John took up his new position in August 1755. He found a boardinghouse near the docks in which to stay and set to work at the new job. Liverpool was still the busiest slave-trade port in Europe, with over one hundred slave ships using it as their home port. About forty thousand people lived in Liverpool, and most were engaged in some field of work related to shipping: rope making, iron mongering, instrument making, and supplying ships with food and other necessities for their long voyages. Walking around the city reminded John of his childhood in Wapping, where he'd been free to wander the streets as a child.

The tide surveyor's duties were divided into two parts for John. He and his deputy rotated through their duties on alternate weeks. For a week, at a moment's notice John would be rowed out on a small customs tender manned by a coxswain and six oarsmen to board each ship entering the harbor. He was called the tide surveyor because these ships all entered the harbor at high tide, and he or an assistant would greet each vessel. It didn't matter whether the harbor was calm or stormy or whether it was a summer's day or a freezing night. Each arriving ship was boarded and inspected by John or someone from his department. No ship could unload crew, passengers, or cargo in Liverpool until it was noted in the vessel's log that it had undergone customs inspection and by whom.

During his first week inspecting ships, John's eye for detail paid off. He noticed some extra hogsheads hidden behind bales of cotton in the hold of a ship arriving from North America. Each hogshead was crammed with about a thousand pounds of dried tobacco. The hogsheads of tobacco weren't reported on the ship's official bill of lading: the captain was trying to smuggle them into England without paying duty on them. This was good news for John. As tide surveyor, he got to keep half the value of the unreported tobacco, which netted him fifty pounds.

The second week of work was more leisurely for John. While his deputy boarded and inspected all arriving ships, John kept regular hours ashore. His job during this week was to visit ships at their docks and clear them for sailing. This consisted mostly of paperwork, and the regular hours gave John the opportunity to explore Liverpool's churches. He hoped to find one whose pastor preached like George Whitefield.

John visited several Baptist churches, but to his surprise he discovered he enjoyed attending Church of England services, particularly services in those congregations open to the ways of the Methodists. Attending the Church of England also pleased Polly and her family, who were staunch members of the church. And because John knew he wouldn't be able to hold onto his job as tide surveyor—a government position—without attending the Church of England regularly, he began looking for a lively Anglican congregation to attend.

To his delight, John learned that George Whitefield was coming to Liverpool to preach for a week during September 1755. It was just what John needed, and he eagerly awaited the preacher's arrival.

Whitefield had preached only once before in Liverpool and was not well known in the city. As a result, he didn't attract a large following to his early services. John made sure he told others about the meetings and invited his landlady to attend, though she responded by saying she had no time for such foolishness. She eventually agreed to go along with John to the final meeting, held outdoors in Saint Thomas Square. Over four thousand people showed up to hear Whitefield preach, and John's landlady was so impressed by his words she opened her heart to the gospel. She returned to her boardinghouse proud to be labeled a Christian and a Methodist.

Throughout Whitefield's week in Liverpool, he and John spent many hours together talking and praying. By the time Whitefield left Liverpool, the two men had become firm friends, and John knew he had found a spiritual mentor.

On September 16, John wrote to Polly telling her about Whitefield's visit.

> Mr. Whitefield left us yesterday morning. I accompanied him on foot a little way out of town till the chaise caught up with us. I have had more of his company than would have come to my share at London in twelve months. I heard him preach nine times, supped with him three times, dined with him once, and on Sunday he dined with me. I cannot say how much I esteem him and hope to my dying day, I shall have reason to bless God on his behalf. Having never been here before but one night, he was not known or regarded by the fashionable folks, although several of them went to hear him. But many of the poorer sort are inquiring after him with tears. . . . My prayers turn much upon the thoughts of our future settlement. It will require both prudence and resolution to set out right from the first; but if we walk with God it shall be given us.

John's enthusiasm for spreading the gospel and for the ways of the Methodists bubbled over in his letters to his wife. Polly's faith was developing, and while she was still too weak from her illness to write back, she dictated letters to John that one of her siblings wrote down and sent on. In one letter, she reminded John he had an important position in town and that he could not afford to alienate people with his spiritual zeal. She wrote about her concern that when she eventually came to Liverpool to live she would be labeled a Methodist and have only the washerwoman for company.

John took Polly's words to heart and replied,

> I much more fear our being cowardly than imprudent. But if we are of the number of those whom the Lord will not be ashamed to own in that great day He will give us a measure of grace and we shall not be ashamed to own His cause and people in the midst of this crooked and perverse generation. But, as you say, there is a way of doing things. I shall try to carry it handsomely to others. It is not necessary to affront or quarrel with any who treat us civilly, but experience will teach you that the less we are connected with worldly people the better.

Before long, Polly had recovered enough strength to begin writing short letters to John on her own. In one, she said her doctor told her she was well enough to travel short distances, so she had traveled to London and was staying with her aunt. She had even attended a Christian service at Moorfields Tabernacle and heard George Whitefield preach.

Then the best news of all arrived for John in mid-October 1755. Polly wrote to say she was feeling strong enough to journey the 140 miles by coach from London to Staffordshire. She wanted John to meet her there and accompany her the rest of the way to Liverpool. John was delighted to do so and was especially surprised when he arrived at Staffordshire and learned that Polly was well enough to travel the remaining sixty-five miles on horseback.

As the two of them rode side by side into Liverpool, John wondered what his life would be like now. Although he had been married five and a half years, he had spent most of that time at sea and apart from Polly. Now, for the first time, they were truly embarking upon life together.

Chapter 13

# Not Fit to Be a Clergyman

In January 1756, the Newtons celebrated the new year by moving out of the boardinghouse in which they had been living and into their first home, located on Edmund Street just off Old Hall Street. John was earning enough money from his job to hire two live-in maids to take care of the housework for Polly.

For the first time in his life, John had a study all to himself. He arranged his books on the shelves, and paper, ink, and quills on the desk. Once he had set up the study, in his spare time he began studying. John arose each morning at five and headed to his desk. After praying, he divided his study time between Latin and Greek. He found Greek particularly challenging. John taught himself a form of shorthand that allowed him to take notes faster. He also wrote numerous letters to men he considered to be his fathers in the faith, one of whom was George Whitefield.

John recalled George's telling him that Liverpool was one of the most difficult places he'd ever preached in. As he studied, John began writing a pamphlet titled "Thoughts on Religious Associations." The pamphlet laid out practical suggestions for how to improve the spiritual atmosphere in Liverpool. When he finished writing the pamphlet, John paid to have it printed. In his journal on Friday, April 9, 1756, he wrote,

> Finished my essay and sent it to the press. I have now to guard against two evils that are opposite, which yet it is likely will join to disturb me: pride and shame. It should seem there is but little to be proud of, but I expect the approbation of some good people may be a temptation—on the other hand I am exposed not only to the censure of the critics with respect to the style etc. but [also] to the blame of the zealots of all parties, to be thought an angry Enthusiast by some, and a lukewarm temporizer by others. . . . I trust the Lord will be my defense against both the right and left hand danger. Let me now remember that I have given bond as it were to the public for my behavior. I have declared my hopes and principles in print and shall consequently have more eyes upon my conduct than ever.

Now that the population of Liverpool knew that their tide surveyor was also a wholehearted Christian, many people began visiting John and Polly, so many, in fact, that the Newtons decided to hold a Sunday evening meeting in their home. During the meetings, they sang hymns together and prayed. Anyone was welcome to attend. John, however, refused to allow the meetings to be marred by arguments over doctrine. Baptists and Methodists might disagree about infant baptism, but while meeting under John and Polly's roof, they had to find common ground in their shared faith.

A year passed, and in April 1757, another famous preacher visited Liverpool. This time it was John Wesley, cofounder of the Methodists. Methodists were a kind of club within the Church of England that was dedicated to encouraging church members to live holy and righteous lives based upon principles laid out and followed by Wesley. While studying at Oxford, John and his brother Charles started what they called a Holy Club and invited fellow students to join them. The club met weekly, and the members who attended systematically followed the actions prescribed by John Wesley that would lead them to living a holy life. The Holy Club grew beyond the university and soon began popping up in various Church of England congregations. The members of these groups were soon nicknamed Methodists because of the prescribed methodical actions they followed in living out their faith.

John wasn't sure he would like what John Wesley

had to say, especially since Wesley and George Whitefield had disagreed publicly on several points of doctrine, and John viewed Whitefield as his mentor. But John discovered he was just as captivated by John Wesley's preaching. At fifty-four years of age, the man was almost worn out from constant travel on horseback, yet when he stepped up to the pulpit, he spoke with the energy of a twenty-year-old. John spent as much time as he could with Wesley, and the two became firm friends.

Before Wesley left Liverpool, John purchased copies of all the books and pamphlets Wesley had brought with him to sell. He studied each of them one by one, eventually getting around to the pamphlet on unethical business practices. In this publication, Wesley argued that it was a serious sin to break an oath. John thought of the oath he had taken when he became the tide surveyor. He had sworn not to take any bribes or collect any money that did not go into the government coffers. Yet John took strokes—the extra kickbacks that added up to a sum equal to half his salary—all the time. *Every tide surveyor did it,* John told himself, and it was true. Not a single man working under John had not taken a little extra money from a captain or ship owner to move his vessel to the top of the inspection list when it arrived in Liverpool, or to ignore the stated weight of a few barrels. *What harm could that do?* John pondered. Besides, he needed the money, especially since he and Polly were now hosting large groups of Christians in their home.

No matter how hard John tried to justify his actions, John Wesley's words haunted him. Every time he prayed he thought of the extra money he made by breaking his oath. After several weeks, John came to a decision. He would refuse to take any more money from strokes. It was a decision that would not only cost him half his income but also separate him from everyone else who worked for him. Still, John's conscience was clear after making the decision. He felt sure that God would help him and Polly live more cheaply.

As John had searched his conscience regarding accepting no more strokes, he had also become aware of another issue starting to bother him—his behavior toward the slaves he transported while he was the captain of slave ships. Although trading slaves was legal and formed the backbone of the British economy, John began to be troubled by his actions and those of his crews toward the slaves they carried aboard. He had seen dark, brutal, inhuman acts inflicted on the slaves, as if the crewmen were transporting livestock instead of people. He wasn't proud of the fact that many times he had condoned such actions, even participated in them himself. He would never forget those actions. And worse was his awareness that many of those things were done while he professed to be a Christian.

John knew such pangs of conscience were odd and out of step with the captains he spoke to every day in his job as tide surveyor. Yet they had taken root in his own heart and were beginning to open his eyes to how involvement in slaving had a way of corrupting men—even him, a professing Christian—to the core of their being. John decided to keep such thoughts to himself while he pondered and prayed about them. But one thing he knew: he would never again view slavery or the slave trade the same.

By now, England was engaged in a wide-ranging war with France and Spain that stretched from Europe to North America, the Caribbean, and India. The war began to affect the flow of ships in and out of Liverpool. French naval ships and privateers lay outside Liverpool harbor waiting to prey on the ships that came and went. Before long only two out of every five ships leaving Liverpool returned. The rest were usually boarded by the French and taken over. It wasn't long before the city felt the impact of this, since almost every form of business revolved around shipping. Stores and factories closed, and few ships left port.

This meant that John had a lot of unexpected spare time on his hands. In June 1758 he took an extended period of time off from his job. John and Polly set off on a two-week trip inland. They visited a network of Methodists and Dissenters around the Midlands and on into Yorkshire. They stayed in the parsonages and homes of Methodists, Moravians, Presbyterians, and Baptists.

When they stopped in Leeds, John Edwards, a Presbyterian clergyman, invited John to preach at his church. It took some persuading, as John had never preached before, but eventually he gave in. The text

John chose for his sermon was Psalm 16:8: "I have set the LORD always before me: because he is at my right hand, I shall not be moved." John wrote out the sermon notes on what he wanted to say and then committed them to memory. He didn't want to bore the congregation by having to pause and read his notes.

When the time for the Sunday morning service came, John felt confident. He walked up to the pulpit and started strong, but within a few minutes his mind went blank. No matter how hard he tried, he could not remember his next point, or the one after that. John stared out at the members of the congregation as they awaited his next words. He had their undivided attention, but he could remember nothing else to say. He stammered a few indecipherable words, but it was no use. He couldn't regain his composure or remember his next points. "Now, Reverend Edwards will conclude for me," he said, waving toward the pastor.

John Edwards walked up behind John. "Continue, my friend," he said, putting a reassuring hand on his shoulder. But John shook his head and walked away. All he wanted to do was flee the sanctuary. Edwards stood for a moment, then stepped into the pulpit and spoke about how everyone needs God's help to do what he feels called to do.

John was mortified by what he had done. He felt sure that he was the laughingstock of the church and that word would get back to Liverpool and even to Polly's family about his cowardly preaching. Right then and there, John decided he would never try to preach again without having every word he wanted to say written out.

The incident was especially painful to John because he secretly harbored the notion of one day becoming a Church of England clergyman. Many dissenting preachers expected him to join them, but he had a yearning to see revival within the Church of England. The only person he had spoken to about this secret desire was Polly, but when he got back to Liverpool after their trip, John decided to spend six weeks praying about the possibility. He knew that several things were stacked against him. For example, he was known as a friend of Dissenters and Methodists, groups not favored within the mainstream of Church of England thinking. Besides, Anglican clergymen were supposed to have a degree from Oxford or Cambridge University, something John could not hope to attain. He knew, however, that the original rule about being a university graduate had recently been amended. He even knew several men who had been ordained clergymen without a degree, which gave him some reason for hope.

Back in Liverpool, John spent the six weeks praying and asking God for a sign as to which direction he should go. As his birthday approached, he was certain that God was leading him to become a Church of England clergyman. On August 4, 1758, a week and a half after his thirty-third birthday, John wrote in his journal, "The day is now arrived when I propose to close all my deliberations on this subject with a solemn, unreserved, unconditional surrender of myself to the Lord.... When I go from hence I shall take my refreshment with a thankful heart humbly trusting that the Lord has accepted my desire and that in his good time he will both appoint me work and furnish me with grace, wisdom, and the strength to perform it."

As John stepped up his study of Latin and Greek to prepare himself for the ordination exams, his friend the Reverend Henry Crooke wrote asking him if he would be interested in becoming his assistant pastor at the parish of Kippax on the outskirts of Leeds in West Yorkshire. This seemed like an answer to John's prayers, and he set out to officially apply for the position.

The first thing John needed to do was find three Church of England clergymen to give him testimonials. He was on good terms with the Anglican ministers in Liverpool and began approaching them for their support. But each of them said the same thing: John Newton was a sincere man, but because he mixed with Methodists, he was not fit to be a clergyman. John was stunned. He knew that Methodists had a reputation for being zealous, but wasn't that a good quality in a clergyman?

John didn't give up. He wrote letters to Anglican ministers he had met on his travels, and he received more favorable testimonial letters back from them. As well as obtaining the testimonials, each Church of England clergyman had to be ordained by one of the church's twenty-four bishops or two archbishops. On December 20, 1758, John met with the bishop of Chester, who was also a sitting member of the House of Lords, the upper house of Parliament in London. After John explained his situation, the bishop refused to make a decision, since the parish in which John sought to serve was not under his jurisdiction. John had no choice but to approach the archbishop of York, an Oxford graduate with a haughty reputation.

When John went to see the archbishop, the archbishop refused to see him. Instead, he sent his assistant to tell him that because he hadn't attended university, it would not be possible to ordain him. John knew this was just an excuse, but the assistant said the archbishop was adamant. The door to his being ordained a Church of England clergyman closed firmly. John returned to Liverpool discouraged and confused.

Back in Liverpool, John still did not have much work to do as tide surveyor since Britain's ongoing war with France and Spain continued to reduce the flow of ships through the port. At the end of 1759, John took three months' leave from his job to serve as pastor at the Cow Lane Independent Chapel in Warwick. John loved his pastoral work in Warwick, and the people seemed to love his oversight and encouragement in their faith. In fact, when his time there was up, a number of members of the congregation begged him to become their permanent pastor. But John could not do it. Despite the fact that there seemed to be no way forward, he still believed he was supposed to become a Church of England clergyman, not the pastor of an independent chapel.

John returned to his job in Liverpool, and a year later little had changed. He was now thirty-five years old and wondering whether his dream of becoming a clergyman would ever come to pass. On November 14, 1760, John Wesley passed through Liverpool again, and during his visit, he asked John to become an itinerant Methodist preacher. Again, John was tempted, but after Wesley left, John wrote him a letter.

> But, however it [being an itinerant Methodist minister] may do for a time or so, I have not the strength of body or mind sufficient for an itinerant preacher; my constitution has been broken for some years. To ride a horse in the rain, or more than above thirty miles in a day, usually decomposes and unfits me for anything; then you must allow me to pay some regard to flesh. . . . I have likewise an orphan sister, for whom it is my duty to provide; consequently it cannot be my duty to disable myself from fulfilling what I owe her. And still the weightiest difficulty remains . . . though I love the people called Methodist, and vindicate them from unjust aspersions on all occasions, and suffer the reproach of the world for being one myself, yet it seems not practicable for me to join them further than I do. For the present I must remain as I am, and endeavor to be as useful as I can in private life, till I can see further.

Unsure of what to do next, John stayed at his post as tide surveyor in Liverpool. He also continued with the Christian house meetings he and Polly ran in their home. And whenever they had the time and extra money, they would help the poor. Things were not working out as John had hoped, but he pressed on with what was before him.

## Chapter 14

# Ordained

During November 1762, the Newtons stayed with Pastor John Fawcett of nearby Wainsgate Baptist Church, near Hebden Bridge, about fifty miles northeast of Liverpool. John Fawcett had been converted through the preaching of George Whitefield, and it was Whitefield who introduced the two men to each other.

During the stay, John Newton was asked to preach at Fawcett's church. By now his preaching was greatly improved from his preaching debacle in Leeds over four years before. Now John wrote out his sermons so that he wouldn't forget anything important, and he had learned to tell personal stories to illustrate his points. During the sermon at Wainsgate Baptist Church, John spoke of how faithful God had been to him through his many trials as a sea captain: the storms, his treatment at the hands of Pey Ey on Plantain Island, and the drama of near mutinies and shipwrecks.

Following the service, listeners begged John to write an account of his life at sea. John Fawcett also encouraged John to do so. Upon his return to Liverpool, John decided that might be a good idea. He began writing about his life at sea in a series of letters to John Fawcett. In all, eight letters were written in small, neat writing that covered the front and back of each page. It felt good to John to write about what he had experienced, and especially to confess publicly that he didn't know why he allowed himself to do some of the things he did to the slaves he transported. Once he had sent off the last letter to John Fawcett, he didn't think much more about it.

In January 1763, John received a letter from a young Church of England curate named Thomas Haweis. The Reverend Haweis was an enthusiastic Christian who worked under the Reverend Joseph Jane at Saint Mary Magdalen Church in Oxford. Thomas explained that John Fawcett had shown him John's letters and now he wanted to add more information and publish them as a book. John was taken aback. Published? He wasn't sure that was a good idea. He was concerned that he might become prideful if such a book was successful.

John and Thomas exchanged letters until John felt comfortable writing his story over again. This time he wrote fourteen letters, filling in many more details from his life. In all, the fourteen letters totaled thirty-five thousand words and were written in less than a month. After John had finished, Thomas explained that the first step in getting a book like John's published was to send copies of the manuscript to various Christian leaders willing to read it and make suggestions on improving it.

As Thomas set to work sending out copies of John's manuscript for review, he was dismissed from Saint Mary Magdalen Church for being overly enthusiastic about his faith. It was an all too familiar refrain to John. By then, thankfully, Thomas had attracted the attention of the one man who could help him: William Legge, second earl of Dartmouth. Lord Dartmouth was the only evangelical Christian member of the House of Lords. He was a wealthy man and a patron who paid the salaries of many Church of England clergymen around the London area.

Lord Dartmouth secured the position of chaplain at Lock Hospital in London for Thomas Haweis. After taking up the position, Thomas wrote to John to say he had given John's fourteen letters to Lord Dartmouth to read.

John heard no more from Thomas until February 26, 1764. He received a letter in which Thomas informed him that Lord Dartmouth had offered him the position of vicar of the Church of Saint Peter and Saint Paul in the town of Olney, seventy miles north of London. Although Thomas admitted he would have liked the job, he asked William Legge if he would consider offering the position to John instead.

Lord Dartmouth had been so impressed reading the letters containing John's account of his life that he agreed to offer him the vacancy. The position of vicar of the Church of Saint Peter and Saint Paul at Olney was John's if he managed to get through the ordination process.

John could hardly believe it! After six years of looking, hoping, and praying for a way to become a Church of England clergyman, it seemed a way had at last opened for him. A week later, John received a formal invitation from Lord Dartmouth to go to London and seek ordination from the bishop of Chester. Lord Dartmouth assured John that he would have no difficulty, since he was acting as John's patron. In early April 1764, John left Polly in Liverpool and took a coach to London. Upon arrival there, he headed to Thomas Haweis's house, where he had been invited to stay.

In the end, John met not only with the bishop of Chester but also with the bishop of Lincoln, in whose diocese the parish of Olney was located, and with the archbishop of York. After each visit, John began to feel he had reached another dead end. None of the bishops wanted to ordain him. He told Thomas and Lord Dartmouth about the frustration of simply being passed from bishop to bishop with none of them wanting to make the final decision on John's ordination. Upon hearing this, Lord Dartmouth took direct action. Instead of relying on letters, he personally visited and talked to the bishop of Lincoln. The next day John was invited to a second meeting with the bishop of Lincoln, on April 16.

As his dealings with the bishops seemed to go on and on, John was heartened and humbled to be introduced to some of the most wealthy and influential Christians in London. Besides having dinner several times with Lord Dartmouth, he also met John Thornton and his wife, Lucy, and his sister, Hannah Wilberforce, and her husband, William. John wrote to Polly, "The Lord has indeed led me in a way that I knew not, and it seems highly probable the acquaintance I have found among persons to whom I had so little reason to expect being known is designed for some important purpose."

On Monday morning, April 16, John again visited the bishop of Lincoln. This time things were more cordial. The bishop asked John some questions about his life and church involvement. John gave him honest answers and explained that when it came to Church of England theology, he was self-taught. For the next hour, the bishop questioned John about his theological beliefs. Eventually, he told John he was satisfied with his answers and the firmness of his theological convictions. He offered to ordain him at his private chapel at Buckden, twenty-two miles northeast of Olney, on Sunday, April 29, 1764.

Thirteen days later, John Newton stood in the chapel at Buckden as he was ordained a clergyman in the Church of England by the bishop of Lincoln. John could hardly believe that his dream had come to pass. Following ordination, he wrote to Polly, "I now almost stagger at the prospect before me. I am to stand in a very public point of view, to take the charge of a large parish, to answer the incessant demands of stated and occasional services, to preach what I ought and to be what I preach. Oh! What zeal, patience, watchfulness, will be needful for my support and guidance. My only hope is in the name and power of Jesus."

After receiving his ordination papers, John took a chaise from Buckden to Olney to catch his first glimpse of the place he was about to call home. Olney had about two thousand residents and sat on the banks of the Great Ouse River. At first glance the town seemed charming, with willow trees along the river and freshly tilled fields beyond awaiting planting. The brown brick spire of Saint Peter and Saint Paul's Church could be seen for miles around. The church dated from the fourteenth century. As John walked up the path to the door, he noticed daffodils in bloom among the gravestones.

John guessed that about five hundred closely spaced mud houses with thatched roofs made up most of the town of Olney. He had been told his parish was four miles long and two miles wide. As he walked down the main street of town, he saw children dressed in rags hanging out in doorways, their faces gaunt with hunger. He passed a few women bending under the weight of the bundles of cloth they carried. Despite the evident poverty of Olney, John was eager to begin work among the townspeople. He traveled back to Liverpool filled with thanks to God and high hopes for his future.

Three weeks later, John had resigned from his job as chief tide surveyor for Liverpool. The Newton house was packed up, and John and Polly, along their two maids, Molly and Sally, climbed aboard the oxen-drawn wagon they had hired to take them and their belongings to Olney. The journey took four days.

After settling into the vicarage, John began taking walks around town, introducing himself to everyone he met. Despite having only two thousand residents, Olney had a Baptist minister, an Independent minister, and a strong group of Methodists who, though still part of the Church of England, held their own separate meetings. The group dated back to a visit that George Whitefield had made to Olney in 1739.

It took John a while to piece together the rest of the Christian history of the town. One hundred twenty-five years before, a group of persecuted Puritans from Olney had set out for North America to start a new town. Their vicar, the Reverend William Worchester, led them to New England, where they founded the town of Salisbury, Massachusetts.

At about the same time, the Catholic monarchy in France was persecuting Huguenot (Protestant) Christians, many of whom fled to England and settled in Olney. They brought with them their varied skills, including the craft of lacemaking. John noted that now almost all the women in the town earned a meager living through lacemaking. The women would sit in their homes for ten or twelve hours a day bent over stuffed cushions on which they wove lace, crossing and twisting multiple bobbins wound with white cotton thread. They left the door open, even in the winter months, to shed extra light as they tried not to use candles that would deposit soot on the fine lace. John admired both their speed and their rhythm as they worked and the chants they sang to remind themselves of their next braiding sequence. The lace the women of Olney made was intricate. Several merchants would buy it from them for a pittance and then take the lace to London, where they sold it for many times what they had paid for it.

John settled into his new routine as a clergyman. He rose at five o'clock each morning to get in two hours of prayer and Bible study before breakfast. "The one is the fountain of living water and the other the bucket with which we are to draw [it out]," he wrote to a friend. After breakfast, he wrote letters and made sermon notes. In the afternoons, he walked around Olney, stopping for conversations and cups of tea whenever he was invited to do so. In this way, he soon got to know everyone in town along with their everyday concerns and questions about the Christian faith. John used this knowledge to plan sermons that would answer their questions.

When he preached, John kept his sermons to an hour's length, about half the time most Church of England ministers preached. He explained his reasoning in a letter to a friend:

> There is still in being an old-fashioned instrument called an hour-glass, which in days of yore, before clocks and watches abounded, used to be the measure of many a good sermon. . . . If an angel was to preach for two hours, unless his hearers were angels likewise, I believe the greater part of them would wish he had done. . . . Perhaps it is better to feed our people like chickens, a little and often, than to cram them like turkeys, till they cannot hold one gobbet more. Besides, over-long sermons break in upon family concerns, and often call off the thoughts from the sermon to the pudding at home that is in danger of being over-boiled.

Within weeks of John's taking over as vicar at the Church of Saint Peter and Saint Paul, the congregation started to grow. It increased when he announced that those who walked more than six miles one way to church were welcome to dine at the vicarage with him on Sundays before beginning their walk back home.

Most days of the week, John walked more miles than that himself. He was determined to reach all the outlying farms. Unlike most Church of England clergymen, John wore his clerical garb only when preaching. The rest of the time he preferred to go about dressed in his old seaman's jacket and trousers, which made it easier for him to walk the countryside.

The Newtons had barely settled into Olney when John received a special package around the time of his thirty-ninth birthday. It contained a copy of a book titled *An Authentic Narrative of Some of the Remarkable and Interesting Particulars in the Life of* ********. *Communicated in a Series of Letters to the Rev Mr Haweis, Rector of Aldwincle, Northhomptonshire and by Him (at the Request of Friends) Now Made Public.* As he turned the small leather-bound book in his hands, John marveled that others would hear his story. He prayed that many people would read it and come to experience God's forgiveness just as he had.

Although, as was the fashion, John's name did not appear on the cover of the book, it didn't take long for people to realize it was an account of the life of John Newton. The book made John a celebrity both in Olney and farther afield. On his afternoon walks John noticed small groups of people gathered around a person who was reading the book aloud. When he got home he recorded in his diary, "The people stare at me, and well they may. I am indeed a wonder to many, a wonder to myself." And on Sundays, people from as far away as London came to hear him preach.

While John enjoyed being the vicar at Olney, it came with a certain amount of financial stress for him and Polly. The salary John received from the Church of England for his services was forty pounds a year, barely enough for the two of them to live on. And then John received some unwelcome financial news. His old friend Joseph Manesty had gone bankrupt and in doing so had wiped out the small amount of savings

John and Polly had invested in his shipping business. Although this worsened the Newtons' financial outlook, instead of despairing over the financial loss, John decided to trust God with his financial future. He wrote in his diary, "It was not much [the money he lost in the bankruptcy], but it was my all. I repine [worry or fret] not about this. The Lord has made him an instrument of much good to me in times past; and though creatures fail, the Lord will not want [lack] means to give me what He sees necessary; but I am concerned for him and his. . . . And are not the promises of the all-sufficient God better and surer than a whole ream of bank-bills?"

The following month, news arrived in Olney that Polly's brother, Jack Catlett, had died after being sick with fever for several days. John and Polly were stunned. Thirty-three-year-old Jack was an up-and-coming lawyer in London. John had tried to talk to his brother-in-law about his spiritual condition several times, but Jack was more interested in making money. And now it was too late for him.

A third letter, which thankfully carried a different kind of news, arrived in Olney for John. John Thornton was writing from London in response to having received a copy of *An Authentic Narrative* that John had sent him. John Thornton thanked John for the gift of the book and went on to tell him he had heard good things from Lord Dartmouth about John's ministry in Olney. Then he wrote something in the letter that made John stare at it in amazement. John Thornton offered to send two hundred pounds a year to help with John's expenses and promised more if John had a specific need in mind. John was overwhelmed with gratitude. Now he would have money to help the people of Olney.

As his first Christmas at Olney approached in December 1764, John set out some ambitious goals for the following year. "I propose to establish three meetings," he wrote, "one for the children, another for young and inquiring persons, and a third to be a meeting with the more experienced and judicious, for prayer and conference."

John hoped to hold the children's meeting in a large, open space. However, the only place he could find that suited his needs was an old, dilapidated mansion not far from the church. The place belonged to Lord Dartmouth and had stood empty for so many years it now needed major repairs before it was fit to use. John got permission from Lord Dartmouth to fix up and use the old mansion, using some of the money that John Thornton sent.

Early in the new year, a large room in the old building was ready for the first children's meeting, held on a Thursday afternoon. Eighty-nine children showed up for it. John used the opportunity to sit among the children and talk to them about Jesus. He taught them some simple hymns. Soon over two hundred children, many of them from the other churches in town, were regularly coming to the meeting. Some in the congregation at Saint Peter and Saint Paul's Church complained that their church's resources were being used on children who weren't members of the Church of England. John didn't see things that way. "When Jesus said, 'Suffer the little children to come unto me, forbid them not, for such is the kingdom of God,' He was telling us we should never turn away a child," John told them.

Not only were large numbers of children coming to the children's meeting each week, but also the number of people attending church services reached the point where latecomers had to stand at the back. Something needed to be done about the situation, and during the summer of 1765, more of John Thornton's money was used to build a balcony in the sanctuary to seat more people. Still, these new seats quickly filled up, resulting in the same situation, with latecomers standing at the back.

The vicarage was also too small for the number of visitors that the Newtons attracted. Once more John Thornton's money came to the rescue, and the vicarage was remodeled and enlarged. As a finishing touch, John had two Bible verses painted over the fireplace in his upstairs study: "Since thou wast precious in my sight, thou hast been honorable" (Isaiah 43:4) and "And thou shalt remember that thou wast a bondman in the land of Egypt, and the LORD thy God redeemed thee" (Deuteronomy 15:15). Every time John entered his study, he saw the two verses, reminding him of how good his life was now and how different it had been when he was Pey Ey's slave at Plantain Island on the coast of Africa.

Meanwhile, John's book had gone into a second and then a third printing. John received letters from people all over England and Scotland who had read the book and wanted advice or encouragement. He spent hours each week answering their letters.

In July 1765 John was invited to preach at churches in London and tell his story. He and Polly traveled to London together, where John preached fourteen times.

In November that year, John was back in London, this time because Lord Dartmouth asked to see him. He wondered what could be so important for him to be summoned. As it turned out, Lord Dartmouth had taken over an orphanage George Whitefield had started in the colony of Georgia in North America and was in the process of turning it into a seminary. Lord Dartmouth asked John if he would consider moving to Savannah to become the seminary's first president. John told him that he would pray earnestly about the offer, but in the end, he asked to be allowed to stay at Olney. He had two reasons for doing so. First, he was seeing much spiritual growth among the people in the parish, and second, he knew that Polly was deathly afraid of sailing across the Atlantic Ocean.

Not long afterward, John and his entire congregation had the opportunity to meet an American Indian—right in Olney. The Reverend Samson Occom was a member of the Mohegan Indian tribe, to whom George Whitefield had preached in Connecticut in North America. Stirred by Whitefield's message, twenty-year-old Samson had found a Presbyterian clergyman who helped him improve his English, learn to read and write, and then study Latin and Greek so he could understand the Bible better. Samson had been ordained a Presbyterian minister and sent off to England to raise money for an Indian charity school.

In Olney, Samson preached to a large crowd and stayed at the vicarage with the Newtons. John was delighted, and the two men stayed up late into the evening as Samson told John stories of how he'd traveled among the Six Nations of the Iroquois, preaching the Christian gospel. John was both fascinated and challenged by what he heard. Like African slaves, American Indians were considered by many to be savage and a lesser form of human, certainly less than Europeans. But Samson's presence in the vicarage stood such thinking on its head. When John looked into Samson's eyes, he saw a Christian man, a clergyman, a man who spoke English well and who also knew Latin and Greek—a man like himself.

Chapter 15

# Change of Heart

In June 1767, after Samson Occum had departed, another visitor appeared at the vicarage in Olney. This time it was Dr. Richard Conyers, John Thornton's brother-in-law. Richard asked John if he would visit his friends, the Reverend Morley Unwin and his wife, Mary, at Huntingdon, twenty-five miles away. John agreed to do so, and a few days later he saddled up his horse and set out for Huntingdon, a letter of introduction in his coat pocket.

Approaching the Unwins' house, John noticed black crêpe draping the windows. His heart quickened. Someone in the house must have died. John soon learned it was Morley, who had fallen from his horse and banged his head on the ground. The impact knocked him out, and he didn't regain consciousness before he died. John did his best to comfort Mary and her two children, William and Susanna, and the family's boarder, William Cowper. It was a difficult time for everyone, including John, but through it he formed a solid bond with them all. Members of the Unwin family all had a strong faith in God and believed He would guide them forward. Mary privately explained to John that she didn't have the heart to stay in Huntingdon without her husband around and wanted to move elsewhere.

Without a second thought, John invited them all to stay with him and Polly at the vicarage in Olney as soon as Morley's affairs were settled. The family, along with William Cowper, arrived in Olney in September. John was delighted to have them visit. He particularly liked William Cowper. Until William's arrival there was no one in Olney with whom John could speak Latin or Greek, and no one he felt he could have a serious theological conversation with. William was an extraordinarily well-connected and educated man who, at thirty-six, was six years younger than John.

William's grandfather had been lord chief justice of England, and his uncles held various positions in Parliament. On his mother's side, he was a direct descendant of the famous Elizabethan poet John Donne, who had also been the dean of Saint Paul's Cathedral in London.

Over time, John learned why William was boarding with the Unwins. William's father had been chaplain to King George II and had made it clear to his son that he expected him to become a lawyer. William explained to John that he tried his best to do so, but before he was able to sit his final examinations, he had a nervous breakdown that led to three suicide attempts. Instead of becoming a lawyer, William ended up in the Saint Albans mental asylum, where he stayed for two years. During his time there, the asylum's director counseled William and urged him to believe that God loved him. Eventually William became a Christian and began the road to recovery. When he was released from the asylum, he was invited to live with the Unwins.

John could see that William was a little eccentric and prone to depression, but he enjoyed his company and Christian insights. While William stayed at the vicarage, he and John met together each morning for prayer and Bible study.

Mary Unwin, her daughter Susanna, and William Cowper all decided to move permanently to Olney. They settled on living in a large house called Orchard Side, located near the vicarage. The house needed a lot of repairs, and John invited them all to stay on with him and Polly until the repairs were completed.

After six months of living with John and Polly, Mary, Susanna, and William Cowper moved into Orchard Side. The house was situated on the village square, and the back of the property was separated from the back of the vicarage by a short walk through an orchard. John arranged to pay the owner of the orchard a guinea a year to allow members of both households to use the path through his orchard as a shortcut between their houses.

Bit by bit, William became more confident in counseling people and praying with them. John was delighted. Not only was he glad to see William moving past his depression, but also William was becoming a tremendous help to John in his church work.

Mary Unwin was also helpful in John's church work. She had a wonderful singing voice. Unlike most other clergymen, John liked to write hymns for special occasions in his parish. He knew the text of the hymns were simple, but they helped children and adults remember the sermons he preached. Nothing made him happier than to walk past a lacemaker's cottage and hear a group of women singing one of his hymns as they worked. And because Mary had a good singing voice, she volunteered to take on the role of hymn teacher. Meanwhile, William began to write his own hymns.

John knew that William was opposed to slavery, and the two of them sometimes discussed the slave trade. John told William how he'd had a change of heart about slavery, how he had come to observe the way involvement in slaving corrupted the hearts and actions of men, including himself. He also told how slowly he had come to see slaves not as inferior humans but as fully human just like him, with hopes and dreams. He explained that daily he felt guilty over his actions while working on slave ships. He told William he wished there was something he could do to stop the trade, but he knew that as long as slavery was legal and profitable, it would be difficult to change the hearts and minds of the Englishmen involved in it.

The year 1768 passed swiftly. In August that year John read about Lieutenant James Cook in the newspaper. Cook was a junior naval officer who had set out with his crew aboard HMS *Endeavour* to observe the transit of Venus from the Southern Hemisphere and search for the mythical unknown "southern land." Soon after reading of the departure of James Cook, John and Polly hosted a nine-year-old boy in Olney. His name was William Wilberforce, and his father had recently died. He now lived with his wealthy uncle and aunt in London. William's aunt, Hannah Wilberforce, was the sister of John Thornton, the man who provided John two hundred pounds a year to help support his church work at Olney. Aunt Hannah brought her nephew William to Olney, and the two of them stayed with John and Polly for several weeks.

William Wilberforce was whimsical and had a curious nature. He and John became fast friends. After the summer, when William returned to London with his aunt, John prayed for him regularly. Over the years, William and his aunt came to stay with the Newtons in Olney several times during the summer. Each time they came, John tried to encourage William in life and in the Christian faith.

The vicarage at Olney continued to be a gathering place for a wide range of characters. One such person was James Albert Ukawsaw Gronniosaw. James Albert, as most people called him, was about sixty years old and had been born into a high-ranking family in Africa's interior. As a young man, he longed to see more of the world and learn things his tribe could not teach him. An adventurous white man showed up in his village. The man had traveled a thousand miles inland exploring and promised James Albert's father he would escort his son to the coast and from there take him to live with his family. There James Albert would be welcomed and taught English and the ways of white people.

Sadly, the only one of the white man's ways James Albert learned at the end of his grueling trek to the coast was treachery. Instead of taking James Albert home to live with his family, his "mentor" sold him into slavery. James Albert was chained up on an overcrowded slave ship and taken from Africa to Barbados in the Caribbean and then on to New York, where he was sold to a clergyman as his slave. The clergyman treated James Albert kindly and taught him to speak and read English. He also gave him a copy of a pamphlet titled *Call to the Unconverted,* written by an Englishman named Richard Baxter. After reading the pamphlet, James Albert became a Christian. When his clergyman master died, James Albert was given his freedom, though he chose to stay with his former master's widow and her children until one by one they also died.

While reading *Call to the Unconverted* many years before, James Albert had gained the impression that the people of England, particularly those in Kidderminster, where Richard Baxter lived, were godly people. He longed to see the place and set out to do so, following a tortuous route. James Albert made his way to England where, rather than meeting godly people, he was scammed out of money several times. Eventually he married a poor English weaver, and together they, along with their ever-increasing family, eked out a living.

John had felt nervous at first about James Albert coming to visit him. After all, he had been one of the slave-ship captains who played a part in capturing and transporting African men, women, and children into slavery. He needn't have worried. James Albert had long ago forgiven those who betrayed him and ensnared him into slavery. John and James Albert spent many hours together, talking about their spiritual journeys and their experiences in Africa. John gladly introduced James Albert to his congregation and urged them to listen to what he had to say.

In late 1772, John grew concerned about his friend William Cowper. William's brother had recently died, and William hadn't seemed to be able to get back to the routine of a normal life. John poured out his heart about the situation in his journal, the three-hundred-page book he had been writing in faithfully for sixteen years. As he neared the last page of the book, John took the month of December to read back through his journal in preparation for the new year ahead, when he would start writing in a new journal. As he read, John was overcome by how far he had grown in his personal faith and by how God had picked him up the many times he had fallen into disbelief or despair. As he read, two verses from the Old Testament came to mind in which King David prayed to God and asked, "Who am I, O LORD God, and what is mine house, that thou hast brought me hitherto? . . . [Thou] hast regarded me according to the estate of a man of high degree, O LORD God" (1 Chronicles 17:16–17).

John was still thinking about David's prayer to God, his own spiritual journey, and how much he wished for William Cowper to understand more of God's grace when he began writing the words for a new hymn to be sung at the New Year's Day service. He gave the hymn the title "Faith's Review and Expectation." It was intended as a review of where God had led John so far in his life and an expectation that God would continue to take care of him and guide him in the future. John picked up his quill and began penning the words to the first verse of the hymn.

Amazing grace, how sweet the sound
That saved a wretch like me
I once was lost but now am found
Was blind but now I see.

Over the next few days, John added five more verses to his new hymn. When he was satisfied with the words, John handed them to Mary Unwin for her to set them to a tune. The congregation at the Church of Saint Peter and Saint Paul in Olney sang the new hymn with enthusiasm and listened to John's sermon on "New Beginnings" at the New Year's Day service. As he preached, John often glanced down at William Cowper, silently praying that the new year would be a fresh new beginning for him too. But it wasn't to be.

That night John awoke to the sound of someone pounding on the vicarage door. Rushing to answer it, he found Mary's housekeeper shivering in the dark. She explained that William had tried to slit his wrists at Orchard Side. John rushed to the house in time to bind up his friend's wounds and save his life. But saving William's sanity proved a much longer process. William confided in John that he was sure that God had forsaken him and that he was unworthy of going to heaven. John explained that all people are unworthy of such a gift as heaven but that the gift is given freely to all. Nevertheless, William Cowper was certain that God was done with him.

John knew that William was unable to think straight as he battled another bout of mental illness. John sat with him hour after hour, day after day, encouraging him to eat, rest, and meditate upon the goodness of God. But things didn't improve, and William made more attempts to take his own life. In April 1773, Mary Unwin and William again moved into the vicarage, where John, Polly, and Mary could share the burden of looking after William around the clock. When John Thornton learned of the Newtons' sacrifice, he doubled the two-hundred-pound allowance he sent them each year and wished William Cowper a speedy recovery.

It was thirteen months before William felt strong enough to leave the vicarage and go back to live at Orchard Side. He told John he was no longer worthy to write a hymn or darken the doors of a church. Instead, he stayed in his house, writing poems and studying Greek and Latin.

John was devastated at losing his hymn-writing partner. In his distress, he too stopped writing hymns and concentrated instead on writing a series of letters answering questions about Christian living. The letters were published in *Gospel* magazine. Although he tried to disguise his identity by using the pseudonym Omnicron, the mixture of scholarship and practical advice in the letters soon gave away John's identity.

Slowly, more than a year after William left the vicarage and returned to Orchard Side, John resumed hymn writing, though he never stopped missing William's creative companionship during the process.

Not long after John got back to writing hymn lyrics, he and Polly welcomed a permanent addition to their household: five-year-old Betsy Catlett, daughter of Polly's deceased youngest brother George. Because George's widow had recently died, the Newtons adopted Betsy and welcomed her into their family with open arms. By now John was fifty years old and Polly forty-six, and they had long ago given up on having their own children.

The Newton household became even more crowded the following year, 1776, when Polly's father became ill and they invited him to live with them at

Olney so they could take care of him. Polly's mother had died three years before.

As John and Polly adjusted to the changes in their home life, Great Britain was adjusting to a new reality. Thirteen of the British colonies in North America were rebelling. Rumor was that the colonists were so angry over taxes levied against them that war might break out. The situation that developed in North America shocked King George III and Parliament in London. As a Church of England clergyman, John was expected to fall in line with the king, who was head of the church. The problem was that John and many of his congregation in Olney were sympathetic to the rebelling colonists. The residents of Olney had direct ties with the colonists in Salisbury, Massachusetts, who had left the town over 130 years before to settle in North America. Many in the congregation made no secret of the fact that they hoped the colonists would stand up for themselves against tyranny.

On May 31, 1775, reports had reached Britain of direct fighting that occurred in mid-April between British soldiers and American colonists. The fighting took place at Concord and Lexington in Massachusetts and led to bloodshed and death, particularly among the British forces. On receiving the news, John wrote in his journal, "The paper this evening brought an account of the commencement of hostilities in New England and many killed on both sides. These things I fear are the beginning of sorrows."

Many people in Olney were afraid of what might happen next. So John announced that he would begin a five o'clock prayer meeting each Tuesday morning, during which people could pray for a peaceful resolution to the situation in North America. He was shocked when early on the first Tuesday morning over two hundred people showed up for the prayer meeting. The next Tuesday morning, Mary taught those who came a hymn John had written for the meeting.

> The gathering clouds, with aspect dark,
> A rising storm presage;
> Oh! To be hid within the ark;
> And sheltered from its rage!
> May we, at least with one consent,
> Fall low before the throne;
> With tears the nation's sins lament
> The churches, and our own.

John knew that he was walking a narrow line penning such words. Rumor had it that King George III would jail any clergyman who spoke against the war or supported the colonists' side.

Chapter 16

# Rector

Over the next two years, the war between Great Britain and her thirteen rebellious North American colonies intensified. On August 12, 1776, newspapers reported that in early July people representing each of the colonies had signed a declaration of independence from the British. More news followed. It seemed the mood of the American colonists had turned nasty. On the night of July 9, 1776, after the Declaration of Independence was read aloud for the first time in New York City, soldiers, sailors, and locals made their way to Bowling Green, near the southern tip of Manhattan Island, where a lead statue of King George III on horseback had been erected.

The mob gathered around the four-thousand-pound statue, tied ropes around it, and pulled it over.

The lead from the statue was cut up and taken by wagon to an orchard, where it was melted down to make musket balls for the rifles of the American soldiers fighting for their freedom from Great Britain. King George III's head from the statue was rescued by his supporters and shipped to England.

The following February *Lloyd's Evening Post* newspaper reported, "A New York paper is said to be received, from which the following paragraph is taken, dated the 30th December, 1776: 'Wednesday morning last, one of the Hessian brigades [German mercenary soldiers fighting for the British in North America] stationed at Trenton was surprised by a large body of rebels and after an engagement which lasts for a little time, between 300 and 400 [Hessians] made good their retreat, and the whole loss was about 900 men.'"

As John read about these events, he realized that the American colonists would not give up. They were determined to win their independence. And even though the war was taking place thousands of miles away across the Atlantic Ocean, it was taking its toll on the people of England, just as John feared it would. Taxes went up, the lace trade collapsed in Olney, and many young men were impressed into service aboard British navy warships. Those who stayed behind became unruly. Gone were the early days when hundreds of young people came to hear John preach. Now they seemed surly and ready for trouble.

As the war in North America continued, Polly's father grew sicker. He died on August 2, 1777, and was buried in the Olney churchyard. John was grateful that he died peacefully, surrounded by those who loved him.

Nearly three months later, on October 22, a fire broke out in a thatched cottage in Olney. The fire spread quickly until fifteen homes were destroyed. John wept with his parishioners over their loss. Those who had lived in the destroyed houses now lived from hand to mouth, and losing their dwelling was an almost insurmountable setback. Knowing this, John wrote to his Christian friends and raised two hundred pounds to help those who had lost everything. He also wrote a hymn to comfort those affected by the fire. The hymn was sung by the congregation during the November 2 church service.

Having witnessed the devastation of a fire in town, John was concerned about the annual Guy Fawkes celebration coming up on November 5. This was a traditional night of bonfires and fireworks which, when combined with alcohol, led to men brawling in the streets. Because the last thing Olney needed was another fire, John took his concerns before the Guy Fawkes celebration organizing committee. The committee members agreed that since the memory of the fire was still fresh, they should not have bonfires on Guy Fawkes night in the town. This made perfect sense to John, but not to the town's inhabitants, who turned on him. They wanted their night of fireworks, drinking, and revelry. And they got it. On Wednesday night, November 5, 1777, a mob of about fifty people, mostly drunk, made their way down the main street of Olney. They broke the windows of the houses they passed and threatened worse if the inhabitants didn't give them money. Sitting in his study, John could hear the noise in the distance.

Soon someone was banging on the vicarage door. A member of the congregation had come to warn John that a rioting mob was headed for the vicarage. Polly was immediately frightened, and John tried to calm her. But the sound of the mob grew closer, until the rioters were right outside. John wanted to reason with the mob, but Polly begged him not to go. She was concerned that he could be attacked, perhaps even killed. John listened to Polly. Around ten o'clock he went out to face the mob, not to reason with them but to pay the mob's lead troublemaker a shilling if he led the group away from the vicarage. The bargain was struck, and the mob moved on.

The next morning John was embarrassed to admit he had paid the rioters to go away. But the more painful realization for him was that many of the residents of Olney no longer respected his authority as their vicar. He wondered if reaction to the war against the rebellious American colonies was making the young men in town restless and emboldened, or had they become so familiar with John that they no longer took him and his ministry seriously? Whatever the reason, John slowly came to the conclusion that his time as vicar at Olney was drawing to a close. Once, he had hoped to die in the town and be buried in the churchyard. Now he prayed that God would guide him elsewhere and send a new vicar to reach the town's youth.

John started the new year in 1778 on a somber note. The hymn he wrote for the New Year's Day service reflected his concern for those who were dying in the war, especially the young men.

Sad experience may relate
What a year the last has been!
Crops of sorrow have been great,
From the fruitful seeds of sin.
Oh! what numbers gay and blithe
Fell by Death's unsparing scythe?
While they thought the world their own,
Suddenly he mowed them down.
See how War, with dreadful stride,
Marches at the Lord's command,
Spreading desolation wide,
Through a once much-favored land:
War, with heart and arms of steel,
Preys on thousands at a meal.
Daily drinking human gore,
Still he thirsts and calls for more.

John continued writing a hymn every week. Sometimes he wrote about grand themes like love and redemption, at other times about specific events like harvest time or the fire. During his time in Olney, John's hymns had grown in popularity. Many visitors asked for copies of the lyrics to take back to their families and churches. Each song leader then got to choose the music he or she thought best fitted the lyrics.

In early 1779 John decided it was time to publish his hymns along with those of William Cowper. He saw this as a way to honor their long friendship. By mid-February, the hymnal, containing 281 hymns by John Newton and 67 by William Cowper was ready to be printed. As always, John's friend John Thornton stepped in, offering to pay the printing and distribution costs of the first thousand copies. The hymnal quickly sold out, and a second printing was made.

Soon after the second printing of the hymnal, John received a letter from John Thornton inviting him to become the rector of Saint Mary Woolnoth Church, at the corner of Lombard Street and King William Street, right in the heart of the City of London. John was taken aback by the offer. He had been praying about leaving Olney but had not for a moment imagined he might end up at a church in the center of one of the busiest cities in the world. He was now fifty-four years old and had grown accustomed to country living. Nevertheless, he prayed about the position and concluded that he and Polly were to begin a new and busy chapter of their lives.

On January 15, 1780, John moved to London while Polly and Betsy stayed in Olney. John's first job in London was to find a suitable home for them all to live in, since the vicarage at Saint Mary Woolnoth had been leased out to the post office. John soon found a place to rent at 13 Charles Square, Hoxton, about a mile north of the church. It was a large three-story house with six bedrooms. The gardens were well tended, and John knew that Polly would love spending time in them.

Saint Mary Woolnoth was a tall, white stone building. A church building had stood on the site since at least the twelfth century. The current structure was built in 1711 to replace the older church structure that had been damaged in the fire of London in 1666 and then repaired, before eventually being declared unsafe and torn down. Saint Mary Woolnoth served a small parish of about 150 houses, far fewer than the number at Olney, but it fulfilled a different role. The church sat in the middle of London's bustling financial district, opposite the Bank of England. Among the houses in the parish was Mansion House, the official residence of the lord mayor of London.

In March, Polly, their adopted daughter, Betsy, and their three long-time servants moved into the house at Charles Square with John. At this point in their lives, they all seemed to John to be more like aging family members living together. Although he realized that one young servant could probably do the work of the older three combined, the servants were sincere Christians who joined with them in family worship each morning, and John was happy to house them all.

At Saint Mary Woolnoth, John's reputation had gone before him, and the church was soon filled with people from across London and beyond who came to hear him preach.

Now that he was living in England's capital city, John knew he would most likely be subjected to various political pressures. These came soon after his arrival in London. The Protestant Association sounded innocent enough, but when John learned what the association did, he wanted no part of it, refusing their offer of membership. The Protestant Association had been started two years before by Lord George Gordon in response to the Catholic Relief Act. For many years, Catholics had been considered second-class citizens in British society. They were shunned and legally shut out of public life. But as the war with the North American colonies dragged on, more soldiers were needed for the fighting. Although many Catholics, particularly from Scotland and Ireland, already served as soldiers in the British army, the Catholic Relief Act was meant to make their service completely legal and official. But men like Lord George Gordon opposed anything that gave Catholics more rights in Great Britain.

On June 2, 1780, sixty thousand Protestants marched on Parliament in London to protest the act. The protest started peacefully but soon disintegrated into a violent rampage. John and Polly were horrified when news reached them of the massive destruction the protest had caused. Catholic chapels were burned to the ground. The Bank of England was attacked. Newgate Prison, where some of the arrested mob leaders had been imprisoned, was overrun, and thousands of prisoners ran free. Entire neighborhoods where Catholics lived had been looted.

In a letter to a friend in Olney, John described the carnage he saw. "The devastation on Tuesday and Wednesday nights was horrible. We could count from our back windows six or seven terrible fires each night. On Wednesday and Thursday, the military arrived and saved the city, which otherwise, I think, would before this time have been in ashes from end to end."

When the Gordon Riots, as they were quickly dubbed, ended, hundreds of buildings in London lay in ruins and over three hundred people had been killed. John was appalled that these actions had been carried out in the name of the Protestant Association, and he spoke out loudly against them. "Are these the fruits of love?" he wrote in a letter to the organization. "Is it thus we would wish to be done by? Surely the Son of Man came not to destroy men's lives but to save them."

As a leading Protestant clergyman in London, John came under intense pressure to back off his criticism of the Protestant Association and instead to condemn the pope and his Catholic followers. He refused to do so, writing, "So far as popery may concern the civil state of the nations I apprehend [see] no great danger from it. . . . I cannot see why a Papist [Catholic] has not as good a right to worship God according to his conscience, though erroneous, to educate his children, etc. as I have myself. I am no friend of persecution or restraint in matters of conscience."

Six weeks after the Gordon Riots ended, news arrived from North America that British forces had taken control of the city of Charlestown, South Carolina. It seemed the tide was turning in the war and the British might be on their way to putting down the rebellion. John hoped it would soon be over. Having experienced firsthand the several days of rioting in London, it distressed him to think how people in the American colonies were holding up month after month as the war dragged on.

Besides preaching three times a week at Saint Mary Woolnoth and visiting his parishioners, John made time for many other activities. He already had a number of friends in London, including John Thornton and Hannah Wilberforce, who, along with many others, invited him into their homes, where he told his story of redemption to their guests. Sometimes he also conducted lecture series in private homes. One of his most popular series was based on the book *Pilgrim's Progress*.

John also found time to edit a book of poems for William Cowper. While William steadfastly refused to write any more hymns, he continued writing poems. The poetry book was published in 1781, with John writing the foreword for the volume. Another book was published that same year. *Cardiphonia* (heart sounds) was a collection of letters John had written to friends over the years. Both William Cowper's poetry book and *Cardiphonia* were instant successes, further thrusting John Newton into the limelight.

Chapter 17

# Stay the Course

In January 1783, at the Castle and Falcon Inn on Aldersgate Street in London, John Newton convened the first meeting of the Eclectic Society with six of his friends. The group's purpose was to discuss a variety of Christian topics in depth. John hoped that over time the society would attract a diverse group of men, including Dissenters and those within the Church of England, both clergymen and laymen.

The Eclectic Society got off to a good start, with members returning each week to spend three hours together in discussion. A topic that often came up was the state of the war with the American colonists. Now that he lived in London, John was exposed to many influential men who closely watched the battles across the Atlantic. Some of them would lose a lot of their investments if Britain lost the war.

By September 3, 1783, however, the war was over. On that day representatives of King George III and representatives from the victorious American colonies—John Adams, Benjamin Franklin, David Hartley, and John Jay—met to sign the Treaty of Paris. The treaty confirmed that the thirteen colonies were now independent. It also settled such issues as fishing rights, what should happen to British loyalists and property left behind, and what to do with the prisoners of war. Great Britain ceded to the thirteen colonies—now called the United States of America—all territory between the Appalachian Mountains on the east and the Mississippi River on the west, which doubled the size of the new nation. John was relieved when the treaty was signed and the bloodshed over. He hoped the two countries would find a way to work together in peace.

As John became better known in London, more and more people sought out his spiritual insights and advice, and he decided to open his home for breakfast two mornings a week. Anyone was welcome to visit the Newton home and eat with the family, after which any man who could spare the time retired to John's study, where they prayed and discussed spiritual matters.

As the years went by, John and Polly's lives became even more busy. The family of Polly's younger sister, Elizabeth Cunningham, was ravaged by consumption. The dreaded disease claimed the lives of Elizabeth's husband, James, and two of their three children, John and Susie. And now Elizabeth appeared to be dying from it as well. And when she died, Polly and John, without hesitating, adopted twelve-year-old Eliza, the sole surviving member of the Cunningham family. Eliza moved into the Newton home, but it was soon obvious to John that she was beginning to show early signs of having consumption herself.

Since Eliza was too weak to attend school, John took her to the seaside for a while in an attempt to help her breathe more easily. Each morning and evening, John would read the Bible to Eliza and pray with her, and Eliza's gentle spirit encouraged him. Sadly, on Thursday, October 6, 1785, Eliza succumbed to the consumption and died. It was a bittersweet moment for John and Polly. While they believed she had gone on to heaven, they knew they would miss her deeply. John preached at Eliza's funeral and wrote a pamphlet about her bravery in the face of death.

Two months later, on Sunday, December 4, 1785, John received a mysterious letter at his house in Hoxton. It read,

> I wish to have some serious conversation with you, and will take the liberty of calling on you for that purpose, in half an hour; when, if you cannot receive me, you will have the goodness to let me have a letter put into my hands at the door, naming a time and place for our meeting, the earlier the more agreeable to me. I have had ten thousand doubts within myself, whether or not I should discover myself to

> you; but every argument against doing it has its foundation in pride. I am sure you will hold yourself bound to let no one living know of this application, or of my visit, till I release you for the obligation.
>
> William Wilberforce
>
> P.S. Remember that I must be secret, and that the gallery of the House is now so universally attended, that the face of a member of Parliament is pretty well known.

John was unable to meet with William that afternoon, and he wrote him a note setting up an appointment for the following Wednesday.

That night John prayed for William, as he had so many times before. Although he hadn't seen William for many years, William's aunt Hannah Wilberforce had kept John up with family news. William was now twenty-six years old and doing well. He had risen to become a member of Parliament and had so far managed to avoid scandals. From John's point of view, however, William had left behind the religious convictions of his childhood and, according to his aunt, had no time for church activities. But John wondered if that might be changing. Why would an up-and-coming young politician want a secret meeting with him?

John soon found out when William arrived at his house the following Wednesday. And although John hadn't seen William since he was a boy, he recognized him right away. "Come in, lad," he said. "I have never given up hope of seeing you again. Sit with me by the fire and tell me what's on your mind."

Over the next hour, William poured out his heart to John. He explained how during the previous two summers he had chaperoned his sister and two female cousins as they vacationed in France, Switzerland, and Belgium. He had asked Isaac Milner, a professor at Cambridge University, to go along with him for some male company. The trip involved long coach rides, and after running out of other material to read and discuss, they began taking turns reading aloud and discussing Philip Dallridge's *The Rise and Progress of Religion in the Soul.*

William related how shocked he was to learn that the book had stirred something deep in his heart. The more he and Isaac read the book together, the more he realized that his own life was selfish and shallow, and the more he wanted to become a Christian. William had tried to distract himself from such thoughts through friends, drinking, and gambling, but it hadn't worked. Now, he told John, he wanted to live a Christian life but didn't see how that was compatible with being in Parliament. He needed advice. Should he give up his seat in Parliament and retire to the Lake District to pray and study the Bible?

John was astonished by the question. Sitting before him was a bright young man thinking of giving up every area of influence in his life. There were times when and people for whom John thought this might have been a good thing, but not so for William

Wilberforce. John sensed that William had important work ahead of him. He told William, "Are you sure it's necessary to give up one for the other? It doesn't seem to me that you must leave one to embark upon the other. It is possible the Lord wants you to be both a Christian and a statesman. Although these roles don't often exist together, they are not incompatible."

William nodded and then said, "That's just what Prime Minster William Pitt told me when I mentioned I was thinking of leaving. But if I stay in politics, I don't know what purpose I would serve."

"You don't know now," John countered. "But we will both pray that God unfolds His will for you. I'm certain He has something important in mind."

Over the next weeks, John and William met together often. William had many doubts as a new Christian, doubts John vividly remembered having had himself. Within weeks of their first meeting, William threw off his notion of secrecy and joined the congregation of Saint Mary Woolnoth, attending services on Sundays as well as John's Wednesday night lectures.

On March 21, 1786, John, Polly, Betsy, and their servants moved into a new home in the Coleman Street Buildings, located closer to the church. William continued to visit John there, borrowing an array of Christian books and discussing with John the important issues he faced.

At times William was discouraged by the slow pace of change in English politics. John encouraged him to continue fighting for just and moral laws in the country. William had already championed two bills in Parliament. However, both bills failed to pass.

Despite these losses in Parliament, John encouraged William to take up a much greater and more difficult fight, a fight that had burned in John's heart for many years now—the abolition of slavery in the British Empire. Although in 1772 it had become illegal to own a slave in England, Great Britain remained the biggest slave-trading nation in the world. And more daunting for anyone trying to abolish the slave trade for moral reasons was the fact that the entire British economy was dependent in some small or large way on that trade. Around 3.8 million of the four million pounds invested in the British economy came directly from the slave-trading business. Lloyds of London, a large insurance group, was flourishing as it insured slave ships and their human cargo. Thousands of people, from members of the royal family to bishops in the Church of England, grew rich from the slave trade. In fact, the Church of England owned the large Codrington Sugar Estates on the island of Barbados in the Caribbean, and the church was not willing to speak out against slavery.

Although it had happened years before, the misery John inflicted upon other human beings as a slave-ship captain was never far from his mind. Now he could see that his best course to help those still suffering under the horror of the slave trade was to throw his full support behind the abolition movement. He would do all he could to help William Wilberforce stay the course as he championed the issue in Parliament, and with God's help they would eventually succeed in bringing an end to the slave trade.

On Sunday, October 28, 1787, John and William spent the day together. Once again, William questioned how much longer he could bear the pressure of standing up for the abolition of slavery. By the end of the day as he and John prayed, William was convinced that God wanted him to play a leading role in the abolition movement, even if it took him the rest of his life to achieve it. He would be the point person in Parliament for the Anti-Slavery Society and anyone else who wanted to join the fight. Certain that this fight was William's destiny, John was right behind him.

While the firsthand knowledge John had of the slave trade was now nearly thirty-five years old, it remained vivid in his mind. And as he prayed, John realized he had a unique voice to add to the growing antislavery debate. More than that, he felt an obligation to speak out on behalf of the slaves. By now John was sixty-two years old and his eyesight was beginning to fail, yet he knew what he must do to help the cause. He wrote a booklet containing his thoughts on the slave trade and some of his memories as a slave-ship captain. The booklet, titled *Thoughts Upon the African Slave Trade,* was published in January 1788.

The booklet had been difficult for John to write. He didn't want to insult the British people or those making vast sums of money from the slave trade. He wanted to awaken their consciences as to the real human cost of slavery. He began the volume shrewdly by addressing something the British government cared a lot about—the loss of strong, young sailors. It was estimated that one in five men or boys who signed on to the crew of a slave-trading ship wouldn't make it home alive. Those who did survive and return home had seen and done things that would haunt them the rest of their lives. John was careful to write only about what he personally knew. He made a strong argument for the position that most of the current wars in Africa were caused by a gross imbalance of power as entire inland villages were stripped of their young men who were taken as prisoners of war and then sold as slaves at the coast for transport to the Caribbean and North America. John wrote,

> Human nature is much the same in every place, and few people will be willing to allow that the Negroes in Africa are better than themselves. Supposing, therefore, they wish for European goods, may not they wish to purchase them from a ship just arrived? Of course, they must wish for slaves to go to market with; and if they have not slaves, and think themselves strong enough to invade their neighbors, they will probably wish for war.—And if once they wish for it, how easy it is to find, or to make pretexts for breaking an inconvenient peace; or (after the example of greater heroes, of

Christian name) to make depredations, without condescending to assign any reasons.

I verily believe, that the far greater part of the wars, in Africa, would cease, if the Europeans would cease to tempt them, by offering goods for slaves. And though they do not bring legions into the field, their wars are bloody. I believe, the captives reserved for sale are fewer than the slain.

I have not sufficient data to warrant calculation, but, I suppose, not less than one hundred thousand slaves are exported, annually, from all parts of Africa, and that more than one-half of these are exported in English bottoms [of ships].

If but an equal number are killed in war, and if many of these wars are kindled by the incentive of selling their prisoners, what an annual accumulation of blood must there be, crying against the nations of Europe concerned in this trade, and particularly against our own!

John wrote eight thousand words, including a description of the terrible conditions men, women, and children were exposed to on the slave ships. Each copy of *Thoughts Upon the African Slave Trade* cost one shilling to buy, but John didn't want to take any of the profit from the sale of the booklets. Instead, he had the printer give John's share of the profits to the

Sunday School Society. Over five thousand copies of the booklet were sold, and copies of it were given to all members of both houses of Parliament.

In the third week of February 1788, soon after the publication of *Thoughts Upon the African Slave Trade,* John received a summons from William Pitt, the British prime minister. He was to testify before the Privy Council at Saint James's Palace about what he knew of the slave trade. The Privy Council was made up of a group of senior royal advisors and ministers of the crown. When he arrived at Saint James's Palace, John was shown into a waiting room. He was surprised when William Pitt himself came out to walk John into the Privy Council meeting and introduce him to the council members.

During his testimony, members of the Privy Council asked John many questions. He answered them as best he could, describing how he had purchased hundreds of slaves along the coast of Africa and had overseen their voyages across the Atlantic Ocean to the Caribbean and North America. He did not hold back on the details, telling council members exactly how the slaves were shackled to each other, how they didn't even have enough room to roll over as they slept, and the stories other captains told him of the sadistic ways they had killed unruly slaves to make an example of them to the others.

John didn't like talking about such things, but he knew that few people had ever had the honor of addressing the archbishop of Canterbury, the speaker of the House of Commons, the first lord of the Admiralty, and the prime minister at the same time about such an important matter.

Energized by his appearance before the Privy Council, John wrote to William Cowper asking him to compose a poem for the abolitionist movement. William wrote back saying he would like to help, but the subject was much too depressing for him to write about. John persisted, urging his old friend to recall the detailed conversations about the slave trade the two of them had engaged in back in Olney. Eventually William, who was now one of the most famous poets in England, wrote a poem he titled "The Negro's Complaint."

William's poem challenged the reader to think of black slaves as people—people with feelings. It was written from the perspective of an African man harshly uprooted from his life in Africa and sold as a slave to be transported across the Atlantic Ocean. Yet while Englishmen treat him like a piece of merchandise, the African man lets the reader know that while they may have bought his physical body, they have not owned and never will own his mind. While he may now be physically chained, he is in his mind free. And with that, he is still a human being who has his dignity. He also points out for the readers of the poem that despite the color of a person's skin, like all human beings they have the same hopes, dreams, and wishes. One of those dreams is to live a peaceful and productive life as a free man.

In the course of the poem, the slave goes on to ask many questions: Does God allow for what these Englishmen are doing? Does He sanction their actions as they enslave other human beings? Throughout the poem, the African man challenges those who have made him a slave. He asks them to prove that they have human feelings, that they are capable of compassion, mercy, justice, and decency.

John was deeply satisfied when he read the poem for the first time. He felt that William had done a great job capturing the essence of the conversations the two of them had had over the years.

"The Negro's Complaint" was an instant success, as were Josiah Wedgewood's pottery medallions featuring a slave in chains asking a simple but effective question: "Am I not a man and a brother?" Women all over the country wore the medallions in bracelets or on hair pins to show their support for the abolition of slavery. The pressure on Parliament from British citizens to do something to address the slave trade began to mount.

In October 1788, fifty-nine-year-old Polly Newton sat John down and announced she had been to see a surgeon earlier in the day. She had a large tumor on her breast, and the surgeon told her there was nothing he could do that would help her situation. She would eventually die from the tumor.

The news devastated John, especially as he watched Polly suffer for six months with excruciating pain. Then in April 1789, her pain eased, but the tumor continued to grow and spread over the next year and eight months. During the night of December 15, 1790, Polly died. John was sitting beside her, holding a candle for one last glimpse of his beloved wife of forty years.

Chapter 18

# Amazing Grace

Even though John's world felt empty without Polly, he continued on with his twenty-one-year-old adopted daughter, Betsy, at his side for support. In April 1791, four months after Polly's death, William Wilberforce introduced a bill to Parliament to abolish the slave trade. The bill was defeated by vote of 163 to 88. John urged William to continue the fight, and four years later William introduced another bill to end the slave trade. That one was defeated by just seventeen votes.

John had hoped that the second bill would pass, but he wasn't surprised when it didn't. Too many members of both the House of Commons and the House of Lords made their money in one way or another from investments in the slave trade. William

Wilberforce, on the other hand, was devastated by the loss and was certain he should give up politics for good. Once more, John persuaded him to remain a member of Parliament and to carry on the abolitionist fight there.

At seventy years of age, John continued to throw himself into his work as rector at Saint Mary Woolnoth.

On April 26, 1800, John received word that his old friend William Cowper had died the day before. For the last five years of his life, William had been living in East Dereham in Norfolk, ninety-five miles northeast of London. John made his way there to preach at William's funeral.

By now, many of the people John loved were growing old and dying. He looked around at his three faithful servants, the same servants who had worked for him in Olney and had come with them when he and Polly moved to London. Even though others found it odd, John treated them like family. He was as willing to serve them as they were to serve him. He wrote a report on their declining health noting the following: "Phoebe is dropping [weakening] and I think will not hold out long, Crabb is very asthmatic. Sally is so-so. Perhaps one young, healthy servant could do as much as all our three; but then we live in love and peace and bear each other's burdens as much as we can. . . . I shall always think myself more obliged to them than they can be to me, and I hope nothing but death shall part us."

The years continued to roll by. In May 1805, Betsy married Joseph Smith, an optician, and Joseph moved into the Newton house with Betsy, John, and the servants.

By January 1806, at eighty years of age, John Newton still preached once a month at Saint Mary Woolnoth. Two curates handled the rest of the preaching load at the church. Once, when a colleague asked John if he thought it might be time for him to stop preaching altogether, since he was nearly deaf and blind, John thundered in reply, "I cannot stop! What! Shall the old African blasphemer stop while he can speak?"

After that reply, no one else was brave enough to suggest John retire. But ten months later, he had to admit to himself he was too old to preach. He could barely climb the stairs to the pulpit, and he kept forgetting the point of the sermon he was delivering. The curates stepped up to perform all of John's church duties.

By now, John didn't venture far from home, although he continued receiving many visitors. One of the most regular was William Wilberforce. On February 25, 1807, William informed John that a bill to abolish the slave trade had been passed by both the House of Commons and the House of Lords. Within a month, it would be illegal for any British citizen to engage in trading slaves. John had lived long enough to see the evil trade he had once been a part of eliminated. No more British slave ships would sail. No more men, women, and children would be ripped from their homes, sold, enslaved, and transported across the Atlantic Ocean to a life of misery. John hoped that the action of Parliament would at least begin to address the challenge put forward by the African man in William Cowper's poem "The Negro's Complaint." His ultimate goal was for Englishmen to understand that Africans, just like all humans, have human feelings and are capable of compassion, mercy, justice, and decency. John knew it was only a start, that the challenge would not be fully addressed until slavery itself, not just the slave trade, was outlawed throughout the British Empire.

Later that year John's old friend William Jay paid him a visit. During their conversation, John had difficulty remembering who he was talking to. He apologized saying, "My memory is nearly gone, but I remember two things: that I am a great sinner and that Christ is a great Savior."

On Monday evening, December 21, 1807, at the age of 82, John Newton died. His body was used up, but his spirit was still bright. After the funeral, John's body was buried beside Polly's in a crypt beneath Saint Mary Woolnoth Church, where he had been the rector for twenty-eight years and had preached regularly for all but the last year. However, it wasn't his final resting place.

In 1897, the crypt beneath the church was sold to the City & South London Railway to build the Bank Underground Station. The walls and internal columns of the church were supported on steel girders as work on Bank Station went on below the church floor. The bodies of those buried in the crypt were exhumed and reburied elsewhere. The coffins containing the remains of John and Polly Newton were transported to Olney, were they were buried in the churchyard of Saint Peter and Saint Paul's Church. There they remain, and just steps away, inside the church, are a series of three stained-glass windows. Flanked by the images of two slave ships is a window showing John Newton preaching from a pulpit. Inscribed beneath it are the words "Amazing Grace! How sweet the sound."

* * *

Today "Amazing Grace" is the most popular hymn in the English language. It is performed over ten million times each year in churches, at weddings, on military occasions, even at pop concerts. The hymn has been recorded by many musical artists on over eleven thousand albums. Yet John Newton never heard the hymn sung to the music we associate with it today. In fact, he didn't even know the hymn as "Amazing Grace." He knew it by the title he gave it when he wrote the lyrics, "Faith's Review and Expectation," or simply as hymn "Number 41" in the *Olney Hymn Book.*

In the years following John's death, the lyrics for the hymn crossed the Atlantic Ocean to the United States, where the lyrics were paired with a folk tune known as "New Britain." This pairing became the version of the hymn we know and sing today and call "Amazing Grace." During the Second Great Awakening in the United States, the hymn was sung by thousands of people in churches across the nation, eventually becoming a staple hymn for Christians of all denominations.

Amazing grace! (how sweet the sound)
  That sav'd a wretch like me!
I once was lost, but now am found,
  Was blind, but now I see.
'Twas grace that taught my heart to fear,
  And grace my fears reliev'd;
How precious did that grace appear
  The hour I first believ'd!
Thro' many dangers, toils, and snares
  I have already come;
'Tis grace hath brought me safe thus far,
  And grace will lead me home.

## Bibliography

Aitken, Jonathan. *John Newton: From Disgrace to Amazing Grace*. Wheaton: Crossway, 2007.

Benge, Janet & Geoff. *William Wilberforce: Take Up the Fight*. Lynnwood, WA: Emerald Books, 2015.

Bull, Josiah. *'But Now I See': The Life of John Newton*. Carlisle, PA: The Banner of Truth Trust, 1998.

Cecil, Richard. *The Life of John Newton*. Edited by Marylynn Rouse. Fearn, UK: Christian Focus, 2000.

Edwards, Brian H. *Through Many Dangers: The Story of John Newton*. Darlington, UK: Evangelical Press, 1975.

Martin, Bernard. *An Ancient Mariner: A Biography of John Newton*. London: Wyvern Books, 1960.

Newton, John. *Thoughts upon the African Slave Trade*. London, 1788.

Pollock, John. *Newton: The Liberator*. Eastbourne, UK: Kingsway, 1981.

Strom, Kay Marshall. *Once Blind: The Life of John Newton*. Colorado Springs: Authentic, 2007.

Swift, Catherine. *John Newton*. Minneapolis: Bethany House, 1991.

## *About the Authors*

Janet and Geoff Benge are a husband and wife writing team with more than thirty years of writing experience. Janet is a former elementary school teacher. Geoff holds a degree in history. Originally from New Zealand, the Benges spent ten years serving with Youth With A Mission. They have two daughters, Laura and Shannon, and an adopted son, Lito. They make their home in the Orlando, Florida, area.

# *Also from Janet and Geoff Benge...*

More adventure-filled biographies for ages 10 to 100!

## Christian Heroes: Then and Now

*Gladys Aylward: The Adventure of a Lifetime* • 978-1-57658-019-6
*Nate Saint: On a Wing and a Prayer* • 978-1-57658-017-2
*Hudson Taylor: Deep in the Heart of China* • 978-1-57658-016-5
*Amy Carmichael: Rescuer of Precious Gems* • 978-1-57658-018-9
*Eric Liddell: Something Greater Than Gold* • 978-1-57658-137-7
*Corrie ten Boom: Keeper of the Angels' Den* • 978-1-57658-136-0
*William Carey: Obliged to Go* • 978-1-57658-147-6
*George Müller: Guardian of Bristol's Orphans* • 978-1-57658-145-2
*Jim Elliot: One Great Purpose* • 978-1-57658-146-9
*Mary Slessor: Forward into Calabar* • 978-1-57658-148-3
*David Livingstone: Africa's Trailblazer* • 978-1-57658-153-7
*Betty Greene: Wings to Serve* • 978-1-57658-152-0
*Adoniram Judson: Bound for Burma* • 978-1-57658-161-2
*Cameron Townsend: Good News in Every Language* • 978-1-57658-164-3
*Jonathan Goforth: An Open Door in China* • 978-1-57658-174-2
*Lottie Moon: Giving Her All for China* • 978-1-57658-188-9
*John Williams: Messenger of Peace* • 978-1-57658-256-5
*William Booth: Soup, Soap, and Salvation* • 978-1-57658-258-9
*Rowland Bingham: Into Africa's Interior* • 978-1-57658-282-4
*Ida Scudder: Healing Bodies, Touching Hearts* • 978-1-57658-285-5
*Wilfred Grenfell: Fisher of Men* • 978-1-57658-292-3
*Lillian Trasher: The Greatest Wonder in Egypt* • 978-1-57658-305-0
*Loren Cunningham: Into All the World* • 978-1-57658-199-5
*Florence Young: Mission Accomplished* • 978-1-57658-313-5
*Sundar Singh: Footprints Over the Mountains* • 978-1-57658-318-0
*C.T. Studd: No Retreat* • 978-1-57658-288-6
*Rachel Saint: A Star in the Jungle* • 978-1-57658-337-1
*Brother Andrew: God's Secret Agent* • 978-1-57658-355-5
*Clarence Jones: Mr. Radio* • 978-1-57658-343-2
*Count Zinzendorf: Firstfruit* • 978-1-57658-262-6
*John Wesley: The World His Parish* • 978-1-57658-382-1
*C. S. Lewis: Master Storyteller* • 978-1-57658-385-2
*David Bussau: Facing the World Head-on* • 978-1-57658-415-6
*Jacob DeShazer: Forgive Your Enemies* • 978-1-57658-475-0
*Isobel Kuhn: On the Roof of the World* • 978-1-57658-497-2
*Elisabeth Elliot: Joyful Surrender* • 978-1-57658-513-9
*D. L. Moody: Bringing Souls to Christ* • 978-1-57658-552-8
*Paul Brand: Helping Hands* • 978-1-57658-536-8
*Dietrich Bonhoeffer: In the Midst of Wickedness* • 978-1-57658-713-3
*Francis Asbury: Circuit Rider* • 978-1-57658-737-9
*Samuel Zwemer: The Burden of Arabia* • 978-1-57658-738-6

*Klaus-Dieter John: Hope in the Land of the Incas* • 978-1-57658-826-2
*Mildred Cable: Through the Jade Gate* • 978-1-57658-886-4
*John Flynn: Into the Never Never* • 978-1-57658-898-7
*Richard Wurmbrand: Love Your Enemies* • 978-1-57658-987-8
*Charles Mulli: We Are Family* • 978-1-57658-894-9
*John Newton: Change of Heart* • 978-1-57658-909-0
*Helen Roseveare: Mama Luka* • 978-1-57658-910-6
*Norman Grubb: Mission Builder* • 978-1-57658-915-1
*Albert Schweitzer* • 978-1-57658-961-8

## Heroes of History

*George Washington Carver: From Slave to Scientist* • 978-1-883002-78-7
*Abraham Lincoln: A New Birth of Freedom* • 978-1-883002-79-4
*Meriwether Lewis: Off the Edge of the Map* • 978-1-883002-80-0
*George Washington: True Patriot* • 978-1-883002-81-7
*William Penn: Liberty and Justice for All* • 978-1-883002-82-4
*Harriet Tubman: Freedombound* • 978-1-883002-90-9
*John Adams: Independence Forever* • 978-1-883002-50-3
*Clara Barton: Courage under Fire* • 978-1-883002-51-0
*Daniel Boone: Frontiersman* • 978-1-932096-09-5
*Theodore Roosevelt: An American Original* • 978-1-932096-10-1
*Douglas MacArthur: What Greater Honor* • 978-1-932096-15-6
*Benjamin Franklin: Live Wire* • 978-1-932096-14-9
*Christopher Columbus: Across the Ocean Sea* • 978-1-932096-23-1
*Laura Ingalls Wilder: A Storybook Life* • 978-1-932096-32-3
*Orville Wright: The Flyer* • 978-1-932096-34-7
*Captain John Smith: A Foothold in the New World* • 978-1-932096-36-1
*Thomas Edison: Inspiration and Hard Work* • 978-1-932096-37-8
*Alan Shepard: Higher and Faster* • 978-1-932096-41-5
*Ronald Reagan: Destiny at His Side* • 978-1-932096-65-1
*Davy Crockett: Ever Westward* • 978-1-932096-67-5
*Milton Hershey: More Than Chocolate* • 978-1-932096-82-8
*Billy Graham: America's Pastor* • 978-1-62486-024-9
*Ben Carson: A Chance at Life* • 978-1-62486-034-8
*Louis Zamperini: Redemption* • 978-1-62486-049-2
*Elizabeth Fry: Angel of Newgate* • 978-1-62486-064-5
*William Wilberforce: Take Up the Fight* • 978-1-62486-057-7
*William Bradford: Plymouth's Rock* • 978-1-62486-092-8
*Ernest Shackleton: Going South* • 978-1-62486-093-5
*Benjamin Rush: The Common Good* • 978-1-62486-123-9
*Dwight Eisenhower: Supreme Commander* • 978-1-62486-142-0
*Frederick Douglass: The Right to Dignity* • 978-1-62486-151-2